with best wishes,

Harriet J. Kent.

ON GALLOWS HILL

by

Harriet J. Kent

authorHOUSE®

AuthorHouse™
1663 Liberty Drive, Suite 200
Bloomington, IN 47403
www.authorhouse.com
Phone: 1-800-839-8640

*This book is a work of non-fiction. Unless otherwise noted, the author
and the publisher make no explicit guarantees as to the accuracy
of the information contained in this book and in some cases, names
of people and places have been altered to protect their privacy.*

First published by AuthorHouse 7/10/2007

ISBN: 978-1-4343-1142-9 (sc)

*Printed in the United States of America
Bloomington, Indiana*

This book is printed on acid-free paper.

FOR PAUL

CHAPTER ONE

The distant figure of a man worked alone in earnest amongst an overgrown copse that surrounded him like a vivid green shroud. He could only just be seen from the narrow-winding lane, which was also covered in bramble-encrusted foliage so deep, unkempt and wild, not unlike the man who toiled in vain amidst the neighbouring cover.

The deep, green valley was shaded from the rest of the outside world. A small gathering of birds were the solitary source of company within the copse. The woodcutter wasn't renowned as being sociable; more of a recluse. This was due to the nature of his work as he was alone for much of the day lest a brave passer-by called out a less than enthusiastic but polite acknowledgement. The woodcutter periodically stopped to catch his breath and wipe his forehead that lay beaded with an honest sweat. He rubbed his shoulders at the same time to ease the cramped feelings that rippled haphazardly within his muscles. His hands were moulded in the form of a grip from the rough wooden shaft of his axe. He continued to labour. His large, thickset frame casting an enormous shadow alongside the trees as the sun tried to penetrate its way into the darkened mass of green foliage.

Not long after, a slightly-built man of around thirty years, with chestnut-brown hair and dark brown eyes, walked meaningfully along Coach Lane. Tall and surprisingly muscular, Richard Norris walked with a limp inflicted years ago when he was kicked by a horse and the weight of the weathered cane panniers he carried didn't aid in his traverse. Some of the villagers had mocked that he had been beaten by his wife when he'd failed in one of her 'tasks' she'd set him.

❧

Richard Norris who had walked past that copse many times, going about his daily, laborious tasks as instructed by his rather forceful wife, called out in reserved expectation.

"Morning Michal… tis fine weather we have today!"

Richard stopped and peered across to the clearing. The woodcutter had seen him but he didn't reply. He was too engrossed with his work. So diligent in his task to tidy and fell trees in the course of a day proving to his employer, Squire Cheeke, he was able to manage the large expanse of dense, thick copse quite satisfactorily on his own. The smell of freshly cut timber was overpowering, yet not unpleasant, just a smell of dampness. But Michal never smelt it. He was so used to working with it all day in that shrouded area of woodland where he was always found, this time to chop down a stubborn oak tree. There weren't many incidents that passed un-noticed by the ever-watchful woodcutter. Many thought he was rude by not acknowledging them. But he saw them; he never missed anything. He reacted like an animal or hawk, watching and waiting for its next prey. That was the game he played with them, those nosey, gossiping, mindless individuals that Michal associated as "neighbours".

☙

Michal had spent much of the morning trying to win the battle against the oak, which gave the strength of an army a thousand fold. It wasn't very old, no more than thirty years, but its stubbornness became more apparent with every blow from the woodcutter's axe. Not unlike its new foe who tried so desperately to end its life.

Richard Norris sighed and continued on his way. He had his own tasks to complete. He had to walk to town to buy and trade some goods. He dare not keep his wife fretting at home; this meant limited conversation with the locals and the people he knew in the market town of Newport. Lord knows what she'd do! He could just imagine her loud, bellowing voice calling out for him,

"Richard Norris!" she'd yell. "Where in God's name are you?"

Most of the valley would have heard her. Good pair of lungs his dear lady possessed that lay within an ample bosom. Such strength in her breath and her nagging tongue!

Richard Norris left the woodcutter and the perpetual thud of the axe biting into the wood, thud, thud, methodical, without rest. He continued along the lane, towards Michal's lonely cottage. There was no sign of life; dull, miserable place with no immediate neighbours. Richard sighed to himself; his thoughts strayed towards Beth, Michal's beautiful young wife. He smiled as he visualised her bustling in the scullery, attending to her daily errands. He felt his heart skip briefly and he shook his head in regret, 'such a beauty too, stuck with a man like that,' he thought.

ℰℜ

Richard stopped along the lane, placed the panniers on the roadside and stretched his fingers that had begun to feel cramped. He looked towards the cottage once more, picked up the panniers and started on his walk to town. He was only a few steps into his journey when he heard his name softly called, "Good morning to you, Mr Norris!"

He spun around; the panniers hit his sides with a thump and made him wince. His mind soon focussed on something other than the pain. There in the front porch stood Beth. She was holding something in her apron. Richard smiled fondly at her. Beth was twenty-four with fair hair and green eyes with a pink blushed complexion. She had a very slender body and was attractively petite.

Richard blinked and returned his greeting, "Uh...hello, Beth," he uttered feeling his face begin to redden. There was a brief silence between the two. Beth smiled as she spoke.

"I've just picked a few apples from the orchard. Would you like to have a taste?" she added coyly.

Richard's heart skipped. He carefully placed the panniers by the side of the cottage and followed her inside. He blinked as the darkness was in stark contrast to the bright morning sun.

"I've just seen your husband in the wood," he confirmed, rubbing his aching hands together.

"Like he always is," Beth confirmed back to him. "Come on, your panniers will be all right there. Come on in," she warmly invited by beckoning her finger, enticing Richard.

He obediently followed Beth to the back room kitchen.

"I've just lit the fire. It's ready for when I bake the apples in a pie. Dough is nearly ready too. Here sit down; rest your feet. Are you going to town?" she enquired, holding on to her dark-grey skirt and sweeping them in a majestic fashion.

"What do *you* think?" Richard smiled. He continued to watch Beth as she busied herself preparing the pie. She peeled the apples deftly with a sharpened piece of iron that Michal had fashioned into a knife for her to use, and cut the fruit into chunks. Handing a piece of apple to Richard she teased, "Here, open your mouth."

Richard did so obediently and crunched on the ripe apple. It tasted wonderfully crisp and sweet, just like his host he mused to himself. Beth smiled in approval. She moved closer to Richard, still swirling her skirt for effect and bent down, her mouth level with his ear and whispered playfully, "Are you enjoying it?"

Richard swallowed hard, he could barely resist Beth's unprovoked advance towards him. She was so beautiful and so close to him. She continued to whisper, even closer this time, "Do you want another… bite?"

"No, I…I'd better go, thanking you Beth. You know…the missus and all and…" He stopped in his tracks as Beth gathered his face with her tiny, warm hands that still smelled of the freshly pared apples. She was almost on top of him. She leaned forward and gently touched his lips with hers.

Richard felt a surge of passion running swiftly through his entire body. His heart began to rapidly thump throughout his chest as though he would explode. He closed his eyes and savoured the kiss. The aroma of apples; the sweet scent of Beth. She drew away from him and placed her hands upon Richard's shoulders. She smiled at him, sitting by the fire, like a naïve schoolboy experiencing his first kiss.

"Now, Richard. I'd better get this apple pie made," she declared in a mock stern voice. "What do you think?"

she added quizzically and planted her hands firmly on her hips.

Richard responded by getting to his feet and taking Beth into his arms, he slowly and gently kissed her back. He could feel Beth reacting to him, so he continued to kiss her, more passionately. He paused for a moment and then whispered, "When is he back?"

She replied dreamily, "About mid-day I think. Why do you ask, Richard?"

"Because I want you...I really want you!" Richard blurted out and he kissed Beth on her neck. His hands edged towards her breasts that rose and fell in a surging state of lust.

"You are a wicked man, Mr Norris!" said Beth, stroking the back of Richard's neck. "What *would* Mrs Norris think of you?"

"I don't care about *her*, she's nothing to me. I want you, Beth. You know that, you've always known that. Then you went and married that, that...thug!"

Beth looked downwards for a moment. She fingered the buttons on Richard's jacket, thoughtfully. She then looked into his gaze and half-smiled.

"But, I didn't know *that* then. I thought you didn't care about *me*, when you married her...I..."

Richard began to kiss Beth's lips once more, enveloping her mouth with his. He probed her mouth with his tongue, drinking in her taste. Beth drew away.

"Come, we've time, Richard. Upstairs..."

"No, it's too much of a risk. Come on; let's go to the orchard. Come on Beth!" Richard pulled her towards him. He swiftly turned and, still holding her hand, they ran outside to the orchard. The ground was still damp from the morning dew, but they didn't appear to notice as they giggled fervently at each other. Beth placed her fingers on Richard's lips, "Shush, don't make a sound, he may hear you!" They fell to the ground still laughing.

"If he can hear us from that wood, I'll be surprised!" said Richard as he proceeded to kiss Beth and playfully fondle her breasts at the same time. Beth started to giggle again and writhe beneath Richard who had straddled her and was playfully holding her arms on the ground. His entire body was laden with a life-long passion for the girl he had, and would always love.

☙

Michal still laboured away. After a few more hearty blows the tree began to creak and groan. The chopping became uncontrollable with the copse strangely silent save the loud grunts from the woodcutter, "I'll get you, I'll get you," he chanted as each cut from the blade bit deep into the trunk, penetrating the woody strands until the final crack of splintering wood echoed like gunshot throughout the copse, creating a sudden rush of startled feathers as birds took frantic flight to escape the commotion.

The tree landed at Michal's feet with an earth shuddering thud. He took a step back and paused, gazing at his morning's toil. He stretched his body and quickly regained his breathe. The fallen oak lay helpless and insignificant now. He grinned, rubbing his shoulder, letting the axe drop just inches away from his gaitered leg, "I told you I'd get you!" he hissed, stooping towards the tree's trunk, his black hair falling round his shoulders. He paused for a while admiring his work then triumphantly strode back towards the edge of the copse. The sun projected his large, black shadow through the trees as he tramped with stooped shoulders. His muscular frame gnarled from continuous labouring with an axe, he was going back towards sanctuary, his home where his story of the triumphant single-handed battle would be retold, or where frustration of the time it took to win would be bestowed upon those who might be present.

He reached the tiny thatched cottage that stood at the edge of the copse. It was in dire need of repair, window frames rotten and various holes in the straw roof, which let the rain penetrate through at every given opportunity. It stood at such an angle that it was in constant shadows cast from the trees. Michal roared out his greeting to his wife, who he knew was busy in the kitchen.

"Beth, Beth! Where the 'ell you me girl? Is me nammit* ready, I've eaten all what you gimme this morn! Beth! Come ere I tell ya! Now!"

*nammit – Island word for food

༄

Hidden deep within the orchard, Beth and Richard froze as they heard Michal in the cottage. Beth grabbed Richard and urged, "Oh my good lord! Quickly, go Richard! Go! Be quick, before he comes out here looking for me!"

Richard ran to the side of the cottage and grabbed his panniers and somehow managed to compose himself as the bellowing voice of the woodcutter shook all around him once more.

"Beth! Beth! Are ya there?" he yelled.

Michal's voice was irritable and impatient. He tramped heavily towards the cottage, each footstep making the cottage seem to shudder with imaginary fear as he made his approach. Its thatch, bare in patches across the front of the roof, with two tiny upstairs windows that peeped shyly from beneath a shroud of entangled dark green ivy, with a grip so tight upon its stone, throttling from it, every inch of life.

Beth's eyes widened in alarm as the continual bellowing from her husband seemingly rang out all around her. Like a shroud of unbearable noise that she couldn't escape from. Startled by her husband's sudden and unexpected appearance, she ran back into the cottage, trying to tidy her appearance as she went. She wiped flour onto her hands from the discarded dough she was preparing for baking and grabbed a hunk of bread from the old pine table, just as Michal's outline shadowed what little light there was in the room to virtual darkness. Tall and foreboding he stood, with shoulders completely filling the doorway width.

"Here you are Michal; take it, tis already for you, my dear. I knew you'd have the hunger of ten men, such a beautiful morning and....." Beth held the bread out at arms length as he snatched it clumsily from her hands without thanks.

"Awl right, less of the weather girl, let me eat in peace," he interrupted, "can't spend the day dreaming of weather. Where's the cheese in God's name? A man can't survive on just dough alone! What's gotten to you girl?"

ᏋᎧ

Beth smiled weakly and turned away from Michal. Her heart was beating so fast that she could barely catch her breath. Michal looked back at her. The local girl, whom he had successfully snared and married the previous year. She had grown up the daughter of a neighbouring farmer across the valley at Arreton and coped admirably with Michal and his arrogant, possessive ways. Although she was secretly terrified of him and what he could do if provoked, she loved him for his courage and determination. He resumed his vicious and verbal attack.

"Suppose its thoughts of a youngster filling your mind. Let me tell you, perhaps you'll be lucky *one day*, when I'm feeling generous, but you'll have to *treat* me well!"

Beth didn't answer. She was thinking of Richard and felt relieved that he had successfully escaped without Michal discovering him in the orchard. Too many times Michal had humiliated her; he knew that she longed for a child. He cruelly taunted her capabilities to look after him let alone bear a child. Walking around her like he was stalking prey, telling her how she wouldn't be able to cope. She kept her fears of his outbursts and frequent humiliations deep within her mind. It seemed normal to her but it made her very weary to be constantly vigilant against his fuelled and unrepentant anger. She returned with the cheese, hastily removing any evidence of mould by smearing the crust against her apron. She presented him with a large chunk.

❧

Michal smirked as he dragged the bread and cheese from Beth's grasp and strode from the shadowed images of the cottage into the bright, yellow sunshine. He sat heavily onto the bank of long, straggling grasses outside the back door. His thickset legs arranged in front of him played table for his food. He began tearing large chunks of bread with sparkling white teeth, like an animal devouring its freshly caught prey. Small crumbs of bread cascaded like flakes of snow onto his torn leather leggings and he brushed them aside with such force that it sent them cascading in all directions. He glared about him, guarding his food like an animal with a fresh catch of prey. He caught sight of Richard Norris walking down Coach Lane to town and turned his head slowly to get a better view.

Michal snarled amidst mouthfuls of bread.

"He's takin' his time aint he? Saw him long time ago, down the lane, when I was in the wood…" he spoke aloud. In the same breath he roared out in the direction of the cottage.

"Is there any mead left?" He spluttered amongst mouthfuls of food. "I could down a flagon right now."

Beth appeared in the doorway. The sunshine made her squint and temporarily impair her vision as she looked toward her husband.

"Don't you remember, tis all gone now... last night, there tis no more Michal. Go the to Hare and Hounds and see Jed, he'll find you some, I'll be sure of that."

She looked embarrassed as she saw Richard's frame slowly walking away. She was suddenly startled when Michal exclaimed, "I said, he's takin his time, aint he? Been *here* as he?"

Beth looked at Michal, trying not to appear shocked by this statement.

"Who?"

Michal looked irritated and replied, "Norris. I saw him...oh... it don't matter. I don't care what he does, it aint important...he aint no threat to me!"

Beth turned away in case Michal would see her blushing as she relived her encounter in the orchard with Richard. She didn't feel guilty. Not as far as Michal was concerned. She was quite a manipulative girl and her manipulation had worked very well on Richard. She smiled warmly to herself.

☙

Michal watched Richard intently, his eyes glared out from beneath the dark locks of hair that grew across his forehead and touched his nose. He watched until Richard had disappeared from sight before he announced,

"I haven't the time to swan about in Downend girl, time is money and if the Squire sees me away from the copse, he'll be docking me pay for drinking time. Get me water instead; I've a thirst that could kill!"

Michal could only think of himself and of his thirst that needed to be hastily quenched.

Beth obediently went to the far side of the cottage to the well and dipped a cup into the water bucket that hung precariously over the edge, the water was clear and sparkling giving even the woodcutter a few gasps as he gulped down the ice-cold liquid, small rivulets ran either side of his mouth in his haste to drink quickly. As he downed the last, he wiped his hand across his mouth, "I'll be back afore the dusk girl," he shouted swinging his axe over his shoulder, its blade creating a brief flash of light from the midday sun.

✿

Beth walked back into the cottage to the miserable, shadowed back room kitchen and returned to the apples and dough. She started to knead and pull at the mixture, her mind set to completing this labour. She began to lose herself in her own thoughts thinking once again of having a child, cradled in her arms, tending its every need, watching it grow. She felt a twinge in her stomach, which made her gasp aloud and systematically clutch it. The pain lasted a few minutes and disappeared as quickly as it had arrived. She sighed as she remembered her daily routine, to ensure Michal's meals were prepared before he returned. She thought of the chaos that would ensue if she kept him waiting, "You good for nothing," he would scoff if his potatoes were too hard or the meat tough. Beth tolerated her husband with great patience. Her minded skipped to Richard Norris and she once again relived their passionate encounter. He was such a considerate man, always keen to speak with her and ask her if she was well. She remembered thinking what life would be like without Michal. Would it be better than it was now? Somehow she always thought it would be. She continued kneading the dough, this time with more remorse.

☙

Unlike Beth, the many folk in nearby Arreton couldn't comprehend Michal's mood swings. Sometimes he was reasonably civil towards them, passing the time of day. Other days he would make them feel so uncomfortable that they would rather pass him by on the other side of the lane, than look into his menacing face. In most cases he would assume his characteristic demonic grin. He would purposely twitch his hand suddenly on the handle of his axe as they scurried past in worried silence. He was not the most popular person in Arreton.

Richard Norris walked slowly onward. Knowing her as he did, he found Beth was the complete opposite of Michal, being popular and well loved. She was the anchor in that marriage. Caring, patient, yet admiring if not in awe of her turbulent husband. He had known her since she was a child. She had always been small for her age, all the other children seemed to grow, but not Beth; she would always be a child in Richard's eyes. Though now he realised that she was no longer a child, but a woman. Capable of making him feel so very special.

⁊

As he walked, Richard continued to think of Beth. He thought of her trapped in that gloomy hovel, slaving away to keep her husband happy with a meal on the table. He remembered the times he had spent in her company, years ago. Beth had treated him like an older brother. She looked up to him, sometimes confiding her deepest thoughts and worries. Richard knew Beth better than Michal ever would. He thought of her in the orchard. He felt his heart warm and begin to beat faster as he remembered a time when Beth and he had been close. Or so he thought. Beth was only fifteen then and they had both attended the local village dance that was held every year at harvest time. They had enjoyed an evening of dancing, good food and ale. Beth had become a little worse for wear as she clung onto Richard. He had decided it was time to get her home but she had protested and, as he tried to calm her, she had wrapped her arms around his waist and kissed him hard on the lips. He remembered that he hadn't tried to resist. In fact, he had hoped one day that he would again be in that very position. It was an embrace full of passion but, much too brief to his dismay at the time. He could barely believe what had happened now. Richard smiled once more to himself and tried to shake the thoughts of Beth from his mind. After all, they *had* gone their separate ways. She had chosen to marry Michal, which had deeply upset Richard. He settled reluctantly for second best, marrying his wife soon after. His wife was a good soul, in her own right. Loud, over-powering but she was always there at home to welcome him. He let her boss him, as it made her happy. Richard didn't really care. He'd lost the person he had wanted to marry; this he kept secret. He would never tell a soul.

❧

Beth would never hear a bad word said of Michal and was loyal as anyone could be. She held a strong admiration for that man, more than he ever realised, if it wasn't for her, well, who knows what fate may bestow him.

❧

"What took you so long Richard, bet you was caught yarnin' again, who was it this time?"

Mrs Norris was always keen to know the latest gossip. Mind you Richard always managed to provide all the small talk she loved to hear. He wearily placed his panniers on the scrubbed table, laden with his purchases from Newport.

"Oh just the Moreys' down Coach Lane."

"Surely Michal wasn't talking to *you* t'was he?" Mrs Norris was intrigued

"Yes," Richard answered heaving the baskets off his arms on to the floor, "but you never hear a lot from those lips. He was just keen on feeding his face and giving that poor girl a hard time." Richard felt a little uneasy at telling a lie, but it was partly truthful. He heard Michal's voice echoing all around, so it was easy to know what was said.

"Poor Beth, how she keeps going, I don't know," Mrs Norris twittered on. "It was once said Michal Morey beat a man so hard he couldn't get up for a week."

Richard had heard this statement many times before. He had never tried to confront Michal, although he wished he could. It was too dangerous, like an animal ready to pounce. He would not stand much chance against that ogre. Taking a look at those great big hands was enough to make men scatter to the four winds.

૮୬

After she had gone about her work in the kitchen, Beth untied her apron, retied her hair and placed her bonnet over her head. She set off to Sullens House to visit her father and mother-in-law for the afternoon. She spent many happy times with Michal's parents whilst he was away at work. It was her chance to enjoy company other than that of Michal's, even though they lived only a mile down the Coach Lane, it seemed like another land. Here she found she was able to temporarily unwind before Michal's return. They were a lovely couple, very kind to Beth, treating her as their own daughter, particularly Mrs Morey was always providing her with extra food, mead and clothing, just to keep Michal satisfied. They never discussed personal matters; Mrs Morey felt what happened behind those cottage doors was Beth and Michal's affair, nothing to do with her; 'not my business,' she frequently repeated to her husband. Although she admitted she held a concern over Michal and his behaviour. A motherly figure of sixty-four with a grey plait tied in a circular fashion to form a bun at the back of her head, Mrs Morey was rotund, happy and the essence of a model mother-in-law. Henry Morey, a placid man of sixty-eight years, didn't hold the temper of his son, much the opposite. He was able to reason and try to tame his son's temper as best he could. He was lucky in that Michal worshipped his father like a god.

༝

The afternoon soon disappeared as they spent the time gossiping. Beth hurriedly returned to the cottage in time to prepare Michal's meal, just as the sun was setting against the grey of the downs, whose outline cheated the cottage of the last strands of daylight. When he returned that night, Michal was even more demanding for his food. He remained tired and irritable as he completely demolished two large plates of greens and roots, meat and a loaf of bread. After his meal he leant back in his chair by the fire and began to relax. He looked across to Beth who was sat quietly by the hearth, trying to darn a shirt in the half-light, she could hardly focus on her work but she persevered. They sat in stony silence. Michal continued to gaze at her. He had a belly full of food and was feeling comfortable as he planned his next move.

"Come here Beth, let me hold you, let me look at you girl!" His sickening grin turned into a smile of a young man, naive and frivolous, longing for lust.

"Come on girl; make me happy in that way of yours."

Beth got up, placed the shirt on the table and walked obediently towards Michal and took hold of his calloused hand. He squeezed her hand tightly in return as he rose from his chair and she slowly led him up the narrow stairs to their bedroom. He followed her as though in a trance, gentle and co-operative. He stooped to avoid the low ceilings as the staircase wound round in a spiral. She led him into the top room, closed the door and began to unbutton her dress fervently. Her hands teasing each clasp on the front of her shabby brown dress, she continued to gaze at Michal who stood in front of her watching every movement, her breath, meaningful and rhythmic as she cast the dress aside, letting it gently fall on to the floor. She stepped silently towards Michal, her arms outstretched, her nakedness longing for his hold.

Michal became aroused by Beth's purity and lily white skin against the shadows cast by the dim light from the half spent candle that perched on the window sill. A cooling breeze from between the rotten timbers made the light flicker and dance. She untied her hair from the tightly scrunched bun of hair on her head and allowed it to tumble over her shoulders and across her firm, young breasts. Michal gently brushed her hair aside and began to kiss firstly her neck and then her face, his large rough hands tenderly clasped Beth's face, his thumbs pressed against her cheeks.

"I love you most dearly Beth, although I may not show it." He continued to kiss Beth.

"Don't talk Michal, I know. I know you and your ways, just hush now," she soothed as she ran her fingers through his thick ebony hair. Tiny shavings of wood pattered onto the bare floorboards. Michal threw his shirt onto the floor, his chest, muscular and tanned. He unbuttoned his leggings rapidly, his eyes fixed on Beth's body. He was in a trance of uninterruptible ecstasy.

Michal's huge body enveloped Beth as they lay on blankets strewn on the straw-covered floor. They made love, slowly and meaningfully. Beth felt her husband transform from the angry woodcutter to a gentle, loving man. He was childlike as he suckled upon her breasts, stroking the rest of her body at the same time. Beth quivered in pleasure, holding onto his thick shock of black hair. Michal became more excited as Beth writhed beneath him; her hair spread across the sheepskins like a sea of flaxen fields. He gathered her face in his hands once more kissing her tenderly on the lips.

"Dear God, what did I do to deserve you? I must be the luckiest man on the Isle."

"I love you, Michal…" Sighed Beth as she glanced upwards to the roof, watching stray cobwebbed strands of straw hanging down, tears pricking her eyes. She blinked them away in silence and kissed the top of Michal's head. She tasted the saltiness of her tears as she thought of the man she had kissed that morning, Richard. Levering herself from beneath his heavy frame that now lay lifeless and exhausted, Beth dragged the covers to her chin and turned away from Michal who had simultaneously fallen asleep. His body splayed like a four-pointed star across their sleeping area. She muffled the sound of her tears by jamming the covers to her mouth. The candle dwindled upon the sill as in turn she too fell asleep until the new dawn that followed.

CHAPTER TWO

Beth woke early the next morning to find Michal was already awake and moving around downstairs. The room seemed lonely and cold without him, and she drew the blankets up to her chin and relived their previous night's passion. She wished with all her heart that this time she would fall pregnant. After all, their passionate nights had not been that regular and Beth felt that last night could have triggered something off. It was like a culmination of previous months rolled into one final push that would hopefully fulfil her dream to have children, but Michal did not appear to be that bothered. It was not a subject that they easily discussed. She looked towards the window and heard a dog barking in the distance. Outside it was the beginning of another beautiful day as Beth watched fingers of sunlight gradually infiltrate into the bedroom breathing life into the cottage. The rays reached the windowsill and the candle, which was completely burnt out, lay spent in its holder that overflowed with hardened wax. Now its light was replaced with a new light, one more powerful that lit all of the room, much more than a candle could dare hope to achieve.

Beth rose from the bed stretching her arms high above her head: She began to dress. She was almost clothed when she heard Michal's foot upon the stairs. He called out.

"Nice out there today girl. I'll be away now, lots to do, I'll be back around noon. Goodbye."

"Goodbye my dearest," called Beth surprised at Michal's eagerness to go to work. She clutched her waist with her hands and imagined they were her husband's arms hugging her, or perhaps Richard's. Feeling enlightened, she turned with a skip in her walk and began to brush her long, flaxen mane of hair. She tied it neatly into a plait and twisted it deftly into a bun. She had a good feeling about the night before, a feeling that she was able to keep to herself, to keep her hopes alive, hopes that she would fall pregnant. Her previous sadness had temporarily subsided. She thought of Richard once more and felt a little confused over what had happened between them the day before. She couldn't convince herself it was what she craved, be it lust, love, a child or a meaningful, caring relationship. She put her thoughts to the back of her mind and started her morning tasks, to feed the fowls and check the goats and sheep.

❧

Being a man keen to keep abreast of the entire local goings on, Richard Norris always found time to speak with people around the village. They were quite a happy crowd, but there were a few who wouldn't care to pass the time of day with him, but that was up to them. His work of bartering goods kept him in and around Arreton and took him round to many of the cottages, so he got to hear much of the gossip. A lot of the locals always asked him about Michal Morey and whether he ever had the opportunity to get inside their cottage to see for himself what it's was like; although he satisfied their curiosities by informing them that had not yet done so because he hadn't wanted to risk it. He thought perhaps he would muster the courage one day to visit the cottage when Michal was there, but a polite "how do" suited him fine for the time being. He didn't want to over step the mark with Michal. Richard never trusted Michal when he had that axe in his hands, his hand might just slip. Morey was probably a God-fearing soul like the rest of them, though he was hardly ever seen at church, only harvest time and funerals.

☙

In the wood, Michal had begun to clear more branches from the fallen oak he defeated the day before. He felt in very good spirits. He even considered it was such a fine day that he might even tolerate some of those interfering villagers. He thought about being a little sociable and visiting the local Inn. These good days were few and far between to a poor woodcutter struggling to make ends meet. Michal felt life had not given him a fair chance. He was never the sort to have much luck throughout his life. So far chances to better himself had successfully eluded him. His dearest wish was to some day live comfortably providing enough for Beth and for the children he would one day father.

෫৩

As the sun climbed higher into the sky, Michal laid down his axe and decided instead of going home; he would wander up to the Hare and Hounds Inn, on Gallows Hill. Jed the landlord owed him a favour or two for all that timber Michal had provided to repair the Inn door after the last melee, so he felt that now it was time to collect the favour.

"Hello stranger!" said Jed in surprise as Michal walked through the Inn door. "Haven't seen you for a while. How's young Beth?"

"She fairs well thanking you, Jed. I'll have a mug of ale," said Michal as he sat down at a large table and made himself comfortable. A few locals in shadowed corners nodded their acknowledgement of his presence in Michal's direction and continued in their own conversations. Jed brought the ale across and laid a mug and flagon on the table in front of Michal.

"On the house woodcutter, for the favour, let's say payment for your time and wood."

"Seems fair to me landlord," Michal replied with a grin, hastily grabbing the ale.

The contents of the jug depleted rapidly and, upon finishing his last swig Michal slowly got to his feet. He felt good; the ale took away his worries and the pains of his aching body.

"Had enough Michal?" asked Jed, as he saw the woodcutter pouring the last few dregs of ale from the jug.

"Thanking you, yes Jed. I must get back to work before the Squire calls by," said Michal as he dragged his chair under the table, picked up his axe and headed for the door.

Jed watched Michal leave. He saw a troubled woodcutter enjoying himself over a meagre jug of ale, off loading his problems in no more than an hour. "God bless you Morey," murmured Jed under his breath, "May God bless you!"

⳺

Michal left the Inn and began to walk back down to the valley and Pan Wood. As he made his way back he heard horses' hooves and the sound of a carriage behind him.

"Ah, there you are Morey! Wondered where you had been. How is the felling coming along?"

Michal turned round in surprise as he saw his employer, Squire Cheeke travelling along side him in his carriage. He immediately but with a hint of reluctance, removed his hat and touched his forehead.

"Good day sir, work is very good today; I've done what you asked. If you'd care to look I'll be only too pleased to ..."

"So where have you just come from then Morey? Damn you man, that is my question!" Demanded the Squire.

"I've been up to the Inn sir, only a few minutes honest, I needed a drink, tis hot work today sir," reasoned Michal, he felt himself begin to panic. He hoped his employer wouldn't smell the ale on his breath.

"Well! You had better get back to that wood now and get on with what you are paid to do. I'm not employing you to entertain yourself whenever you think fit, let alone drink in my time! What an outrage! Drive on!" the Squire bellowed to his driver. The carriage moved off in a cloud of dust that showered Michal like a whirlwind. The carriage disappeared at great speed towards Newport.

"You...you...urgh!" yelled Michal throwing his hat to the ground "I'd like to see you do an honest day's labour... you!"

∞

He clenched the shaft of his axe with determination and its blade gave off a sudden glint of shining metal. Outraged, he stormed back into the wood; brambles caught his legs as he blindly stamped through the undergrowth. He aimed his axe at anything that got in his way. The effects of the ale were beginning to take hold as he repeatedly cursed aloud. He detested being made to look small by anyone. He was not a man who could easily forgive and he had a dreadful habit of bearing grudges for a very long time. This was one grudge he would not be prepared to shake off that easily. It was not as though he spent his life at the Inn, just the one time, only a short time, and the Squire just happened to be passing by. Perhaps one of the locals had made him aware. Typical; they couldn't keep their mouths shut sometimes. Michal would make sure that whoever had told Squire Cheeke where he had been, they would pay and dearly! Fortunately for him, Michal didn't catch sight of the informant who had kindly *tipped off* his whereabouts to the Squire and, luckily for Richard Norris, who had left the Inn shortly after Michal, he turned and walked in the opposite direction from the woodcutter.

☙

As dusk began to fall Michal's mood had improved. He had taken his spite out on some unsuspecting trees and the ale had gradually worn off. He had torn branches from the trunks of hazel and ash with his bare hands imagining them to be the limbs of the Squire. He felt calmer and his temper had slowly mellowed to a feeling of annoyance rather than rage. He thought of Beth at the cottage busily preparing his meal. He smiled to himself and decided to call it a day.

When he arrived at the cottage however, Beth was not there. Michal immediately became angered and his mood swung back into a rage. How dare she? There

29

was no meal. How dare she not be at home to greet him. He stormed into the kitchen. It was in darkness, the fire held onto a few glowing embers and the table lay empty. He furiously lit a candle and put it on the table, the flame flickered violently as the candlestick tried to hold its balance on the wooden surface sending eerie shadows dancing around the walls and ceiling. Hunger always made Michal irritable, this was too much for him as he stormed out of the cottage and set off to Sullens, to his parent's house. That would be the only place he could think of that Beth might be.   On arrival outside the house, he saw a light shining from the parlour so at the top of his voice bellowed," Beth! Beth! Where are you, girl?"

"For goodness sake Michal, come in and stop making such a noise," called his mother in annoyance from the doorway.

"Where is Beth? Why is she here so late? She should be at 'ome with me!" demanded Michal, his eyes glazed and full of anger.

"She has not been feeling well today that is why she is here. Listen, I have food for you in the kitchen." She ushered him inside.

Mary Morey bustled around the hallway. Her grey hair peeked out in haphazard strands from beneath her starched white cap. Her complexion was ruddy and her nose was round and filled her face in a motherly fashion. She had a slight stoop which enticed her skirts to tip up at the back and drag at the front. She was a busy person, kind and very caring. She loved her son as much she did her other offspring, but she hated his temper.

༄

Michal walked toward the kitchen. His father was sat quietly by the hearth filling his clay pipe.

"How are you son? The ale is good tonight by the way."

Henry Morey lit his pipe and sucked the tobacco into reddish embers amidst a spiral of white smoke. The room filled with its aroma. He ran gnarled fingers through his thick grey hair and sat back in his chair. Taking the pipe from between his clenched yellowed teeth, he gazed at Michal through blue-grey eyes. He was an ageing farmer who looked much older than his sixty-eight years. Henry had had a hard life labouring at Sullens, his body was the evidence of life spent in all weathers, wrestling animals and toiling hard on the land. He continually ached from the arthritis that had penetrated his entire body.

"I am well, Father," said Michal as he sat at the table and began to devour everything within arm's reach.

"Are you not even going to ask how Beth is fairing?" asked Henry Morey in surprise.

"There aint nothin' wrong with the girl, not that I know at any rate," replied Michal with his mouth full of food. He ate greedily whilst his father watched him intently.

"It would be nice to hear you ask, it does not take much for heaven's sake!" announced Mrs Morey. She despaired frequently with her youngest son. She often wondered who he turned after for his *caring attitude* that seemed to evade his mind at all times. She looked over to her husband for support; he only looked back in helpless silence and shrugged his shoulders.

After his meal, Michal dragged himself away from the table and went upstairs to see Beth. She lying on a large comfortable bed, she looked pale and drawn.

"Come on girl, what's the matter. You were fine this morning when I left."

"I'm so sorry Michal; I started to feel poorly a-mid morning. Each time I try to move now I feel worse," whispered Beth trying to lift herself up from the bed.

"Poor girl was on her knees by the time she got here Michal; Lord knows where she found the strength to stagger along the lane." Mrs Morey tried to calm her son.

"I'll get you home, you'll feel better then," said Michal as he drew back the bedclothes and tried to sit Beth upright. His mother stopped him immediately.

"No Michal, leave Beth alone. I think she ought to have the doctor see her, to find out what is wrong."

"But she can't be that sick, I mean we only...." Michal broke off remembering their passionate night. He looked first at Beth and then his mother.

He finally spoke. "Dunno why you needs the doctor, I'll take you home now, have a sleep, do ya the world of good, it will."

He stepped towards the bed to help Beth get up.

"No, Michal, leave her be, she feels too weak to move now!" Warned Mrs Morey, "Leave her to rest and go sit with your father downstairs?"

"She's coming back with me now I tell ya!" He glared angrily back at his mother, making her start at his outburst.

"I tell you you'll be sorry my boy, she may get worse, no one to look after her there. I know damn well you won't help her, poor child, don't you see she is sick for the Lord's sake!" Mrs Morey turned away from Beth as she felt tears stinging her eyes and her face begin to redden. Michal scooped Beth into his arms, heaving her from the bed with a grunt.

"Outta the way!" He snarled, "Out Mother, outta me way!"

❧

Mrs Morey stood aside letting Michal struggle past her, Beth lay slumped in his arms, her hair had fallen across her face like a shroud. She looked very pale and lifeless. Mrs Morey stopped him.

"I'm sorry Beth, I'll be straight round to the cottage, make you comfortable my love!" she soothed as the poor girl was bundled unceremoniously out of the front door.

Michal again glared at his mother and her attempts to interfere with his wife. He couldn't understand why Beth had to be away from home when she was ill. Home was the place to be.

"You just take care of her Michal, you hear me!" Mrs Morey called from the house.

"I wish you would stop your fretting mother, leave us be can't you?"

"Mary! That's enough now." Henry Morey stood at the bottom of the stairs looking towards his wife. He shook his head in remorse as Michal walked down the path.

"We'll see you later boy," he called out. "Keep her warm. You get well young Beth and we'll see you in the morn!"

"Yes father, see you on the morrow mebbe," Michal nodded acknowledging his father respectively.

❧

When they arrived back to the cottage, Michal slumped up the narrow stairs. Beth's weight was seemingly increasing with every step as he trudged his way upstairs. He gently laid Beth onto the bed and pulled the blankets and skins over her. She hardly made a sound but lay quietly as though she had been drugged. She felt no control over her body whatsoever; it was as though she had been cocooned into a tight shell with no space left to move.

"You sleep girl, sleep well," Michal whispered pushing a strand of hair away from her eyes. Beth blinked and opened her eyes, briefly focussing on Michal who had knelt by the side of the bed; the floorboards creaked as he adjusted his knees on them for comfort.

"Thank you Michal, I'll sleep now just as you say," she mumbled and drifted off into a dreamless slumber.

The following morning Mrs Morey called early to the cottage. Michal had already left for work leaving Beth lying alone upstairs.

"Oh dear lord, how are you poor Beth, how could he leave you like this. Do you feel any better my love?" Mrs Morey was concerned that her condition had not improved.

"Hello Mary. I do perhaps feel a little better, but still weak. Michal went a while ago, took some nammit, with him all right, I think." Her face showed concern over Michal having adequate food supply.

"Don't you fret over that one, I'll keep him in food; don't you worry. That'll keep him happy for sure," she mused thinking of her son.

"I take it you've not eaten a crumb? Do you need water, Beth?"

"Yes, I feel I have a thirst," Beth began to slowly stretch herself to get comfortable.

"Right, I'll fetch some water, what about food, try some broth perhaps?" Mrs Morey tried to coax her to eat. "You'll feel better with food inside you for sure."

"Whatever you think is best." Beth felt too weak to argue that she really didn't feel hungry but tried to humour her mother in law's concern.

ᛒᚱ

Mrs Morey made her way carefully down the stairs, with each step she felt the hem of her skirts catch underneath her feet and she cursed under her breath. When she reached the kitchen she winced at the state Michal had left it in. Stale bread was strewn across the floor, meat was left to fester on the table and she shuddered as the sudden movement of adult rat scampered slyly into a dark corner. She shivered as the cottage's atmosphere chilled her. Small wonder Beth had taken ill, just living in such a hole must have brought on her illness. She sighed and braced herself as she tidied away the mess and set about concocting her 'miracle broth' as she liked to call it. 'Always makes them feel better,' she mused to herself. A little later, with the aroma of freshly made broth, Mrs Morey returned to Beth's bedside.

"Here you are my lovely, this will perk you up, try this." She drove the spoon deep into the steaming broth and held it to Beth's lips.

"Thank you Mary, you're so good to me, thanking you for comin' here, for your help." Beth took a few more mouthfuls of broth then lay back on the bed.

Mary smiled down at the frail little body with sympathy, "Try some water girl, that'll help you too."

Beth's spindly fingers clutched at the glass of water and as she sipped, its chill made her shudder as it slowly descended down her throat.

"Do you want any more broth dear, you've 'ardly touched it, it'll build your strength, make you better?"

Mary made it sound as though it really was a miracle cure.

"I've taken enough thank you; I feel the need to sleep now."

"Fair enough, I'll leave you be for the morn but I'll be back afore the dusk, make sure you're all right and don't worry about him, I'll bring him some food for tonight, don't you fret just get well, you hear me?"

૭ఎ

Mary left Beth dozing. As she closed the cottage door, she could not help but worry for one so young she held such a poor record of illness. The next few days passed and Beth showed little sign of improving. Mary Morey had become increasingly worried, convinced the broth would do the trick she decided to confront Michal. Late one afternoon she found him slumped by the hearth, the fire showing no signs of heat. Beth still lay upstairs. She laid her basket on to the table in the back kitchen and, folding her arms in defiance, spoke to son.

"Michal, she aint getting any better, I think the doctor should see her," she declared.

Michal seemed concerned over his mother's words.

"Do you think she is really that bad then?" he asked scratching his head as he moved to get comfortable in his chair.

"Well, she has no fever, no sign of anything really, that's what really worries me. She just lays there helpless,

37

she's been up there for close on a five day now, surely you must know that aint right?"

"Mebbe you're right then." Michal got up and walked round the room "I had no idea she be that bad. I just thought she was tired, I didn't think…"

"I'll send for the doctor now," Mary decided for her son. She walked towards the door, stopped and said, "Oh and Michal, I think it best Beth stays at Sullens for a while, best for the doctor to see her at our place, what do you say?"

"But she's all right upstairs aint she? Won't do her bit a good to be moved." Michal's face became quite concerned.

"It may help her get better," Mary reached out and touched Michal's arm.

"Oh whatever you want, Mother, whatever you want." He finally conceded, "Come on let's get her down here and take her to Sullens. Then I'll go see about getting the doctor."

ᘓ

Richard Norris never saw much of Michal Morey but he certainly was in a rush when he saw him later that morning. He was heading for the Doctors house in Arreton as he passed him in Church Lane when he had called out "good afternoon." Michal had just ignored Richard's presence. Richard thought he must have had a lot on his mind, as normal. Word had it that Beth had been taken ill, been in bed for a week he had learned.

Naturally, he was very concerned but was not able to show this emotion for fear of causing unnecessary attention to himself. He decided that he would go over to the cottage to visit her. Old mother Morey had been seen to visit the cottage more than once a day with food for them as well. Richard decided he ought to go as soon as he could. She was probably suffering the effects of living with Morey, either that or he had taken a hand to her. He watched Michal stride off down the lane to the copse to work and he set off at a quickened pace to visit Beth.

❧

He reached the cottage and found the door to be on the latch. He called out a 'hello' in case Mary Morey was there but no reply was forthcoming. He moved slowly in the dark hall and climbed the stairs. He found Beth lying on the bed; her eyes were open.

"Hello, my lovely girl. What's been happening to you then?" he soothed as he knelt down at Beth's side. He produced a small white flower that he had picked in the lane.

"Oh, Richard. How kind of you to call," Beth breathed to him. She smiled at the flower and his look of concern. "Don't you fret about me, my love. I just feel under the weather, you know. Pains and such, don't know what it is…"

"Oh, Beth," Richard sighed. "He aint hurt you has he? Not taken a fist to you?"

"No, he hasn't touched me. No, I feel a pain inside," replied Beth weakly. "Just need to get better now. Michal's gone to the Doctor's house. They're taking me to Sullens today."

"That's good it's much better there than this place and yes… I saw him. That's why I'm here, I knew he wouldn't be. It was the only chance I had to see you," Richard whispered and laid a gentle kiss on Beth's brow. "You got to get well, girl. I need you to get well, you hear?"

"I hear you, Richard. Now, you'd better be away, he'll be back here soon," Beth warned.

❦

Richard carefully removed a strand of Beth's hair that had fallen across her eye. She smiled and placed her hand on his, feeling his warmth.

"Beth, I truly love you…" he began

Beth stopped him. "Shush now, Richard. I love you dearly too, but you know I'll never be able to escape from Michal…."

Richard interrupted her. "You would if he was no longer around," he pronounced in a serious voice.

"What do you mean by that?" Beth suddenly looked at him in puzzlement.

"If he weren't around, alive…here….breathing."

"Kill him you mean? That's what you mean?" Beth continued to ask. "How could you do that?"

"I don't know," Richard answered. "It, it… was just a thought… a desperate thought. I don't want him near you, you know that, Beth. I can't even think of you with…him…"

"Don't think about him, just think of us," Beth suggested.

"But I want *you*. I want to be with you, I don't want us to be secret," Richard became unrealistic.

"What about your wife? What will you do about her?" Beth was a little unnerved by Richard's outburst.

"She won't miss me; you should know that by now. She'd manage on her own all right."

"Don't she want children?" Beth asked, stroking Richard's hand.

"No, she doesn't. Don't know why she bothered to marry me," Richard said remorsefully and laid his head on Beth's breast searching for comfort. He swallowed slowly and spoke softly.

"Just remember what I said to you the other time, you know…when we…" Richard felt embarrassed. He continued, "That I care for you, a lot. That I ….you know," he stuttered.

"Yes, I know, Richard. Take yourself away now," Beth held out her hand for him to hold. He took it and kissed it gently. Her hand felt cold and clammy almost lifeless. He smiled and quickly descended the stairs and back out into the lane.

સ્

"How long does it take for a doctor to tell ya what's wrong with someone? He's been up there for an age," Michal was prowling around the parlour at Sullens, shuffling his feet, holding his hands behind his back, puffing on one of his father's pipes, with smoke billowing around him like a mist. Beth had arrived there earlier that morning, aided by Michal and his parents.

"As long as it takes son," replied Henry with his pipe clenched tightly in his mouth. Spirals of smoke hid his face as the room resembled a mass of opaqueness. Michal gazed toward the fire. He noticed a piece of oak burning in the hearth.

"I cut down a beauty t'other day Father, oak it was. Trunk the size of three horses!"

There was a noise at the top of the stairs and the sound of footsteps.

"Michal, you can come upstairs now," called the Doctor. "I have news for you."

Michal ran up the stairs to the small landing where the doctor stood.

"Good news in fact. Beth is with child. I may add that she is very, very weak at the moment, so she needs a lot of care and attention. I have asked Mrs Morey to accommodate her here for at least a month so she can endure complete bed rest. It is essential for both Beth and the baby's health. I hope you understand all this."

The doctor finished his sentence with a frown.

Michal looked shocked, "Yes, I understand Doctor," he said dazed. Words were swimming around in his head like a tidal wave of confusion.

"I'll be away now; I bid you and your good lady goodnight. Good night Henry, Mrs Morey."

"Goodnight Doctor and thank you," said Mrs Morey as she closed the front door behind him. She smiled broadly as she saw her son walking down the stairs,

"Well it is good news Michal. You are going to be a father. Hopefully it will calm you down now you have a child to think about," smiled his mother, as she caught sight of Henry who stood speechless but with a beaming face.

❧

Michal climbed back up the stairs and found Beth lying on the bed. There were tears in her eyes, tears of joy and relief.

"Oh Michal, can you believe it!"

Beth had a little colour in her cheeks but she was still weak.

"Well done girl, well done." He leant closer to her and whispered," I told you I'd give you what you wanted din' I? You must get some rest now. Get your strength back. When's it coming?" he soothed, stroking her hair rhythmically as he spoke with his rough hand.

"I am so pleased you are happy, Michal. You don't know what this means to me. Doctor says I'm a few weeks gone already, so it'll be the winter time," she sighed in contentment. Her mind channelled her thoughts towards Richard and how he would react to her news. She felt he had a right to know of her well-being and her news. Somehow she hoped she would be the one to tell him and that he would not hear it from anyone else.

"Rest now; I'll be off back to the cottage. See you tomorrow girl, goodnight." Michal kissed the top of Beth's head.

"Night Michal, may god bless you, my dearest." Beth watched Michal walk out of the room and the smile that appeared on his face.

⁌

Michal left Sullens shortly after the doctor. He made his way slowly back to the cottage, thinking about the news of the child. The lane was deserted and very quiet with only the distant evensong from a blackbird breaking the silence of the dusk. He started to think of his forthcoming child. He smiled and saying to himself with an arrogant contentment," Hope it's a nipper!"

CHAPTER THREE

Beth spent the following weeks staying at Sullens. She regained some of her strength. The pains had subsided and the constant feeling of being tired had abated, so she was able to return back to her own home. She packed her few belongings in a pannier and looked toward Mary Morey; she smiled at her.

"I could not have got better without you. You're just so kind to me and Michal of course, looking out for his needs as well. I don't know however I can repay your kindness, Mary."

"You've no need Beth, just giving me a grandchild will be the best repayment of all. No need to fret about repaying and all that, you keep your health and look forward to the babe," Mary replied smiling at Beth who was almost close to tears.

"Come here, come now," Mary held Beth close and stroked her head that was bent forward, trying to disguise the tears. "You go now, get back to that son of mine afore he misses you even more!"

"Good day to you Mary, may God bless your kind heart." Beth left Sullens with mixed feelings. As she walked down the narrow path and began her short journey back through the lane, she felt the loss of closeness that she always seemed to show Mr and Mrs Morey, a closeness that had never blossomed in her relationship with Michal at the cottage. She felt sad to never have felt this with Michal. As she walked she saw a familiar figure walking in the opposite direction. A figure she knew well. Richard walked up to her and greeted her with a kiss on the cheek.

"Beth! You are out and about! How are you now?" he asked in excitement. Beth looked at Richard and felt it was the ideal time to announce her news. She took his hand in hers,

"Richard, I am better now and I know what was wrong with me."

Richard still looked excited, waiting for the answer; he assisted her, "Yes, and…?"

Beth looked him in the eyes, "Richard. I am with child… Michal's child. It will be born in the winter," she replied and looked to the ground, waiting for his response.

Richard released his hand from Beth's and stepped away. "Richard, please… say something to me?" pleaded

Beth; she began to feel awkward and upset at his sudden reaction.

He turned and looked at her.

"What do you expect me to say…? Well done?" He turned away from Beth and kicked the loose stones on the lane. "I would be so much more joyful if it were mine. How do you know I am not the father? If I am not, I cannot be happy for *him!*"

Beth stood watching Richard continue to kick the stones, his hands behind his back, hidden beneath the tails of his coat. Sensing a feeling of regret, she turned and faced Richard. She touched his shoulder with her hand.

"Please, don't be this way, Richard. You know it is what I desired the most. I wish…I wish the child had been yours, truly I do, but I don't know that it is. It's his and I can't do anything about it!"

Richard looked Beth in the eye, "Do you really wish it had been *me* to father the child? Or is it something you're saying to make me feel better? Beth, I thought you cared for me…about us…not him! What about the time in the orchard? Don't you think it could be mine?"

"Richard, you know what it's like…I'm married to him, not you, I…I'm sorry," Beth wailed, feeling tears welling up in her eyes she started on her way back to the cottage, leaving Richard standing looking after her, with tears filling his eyes and slowly spilling over on to his cheeks as he watched his love disappear back to the woodcutter.

Michal was in the cottage and he heard Beth's footsteps outside the cottage door.

"Beth, here you are girl, nice to have you back for meself again, don't like sharing you, not even with Mother!"

Beth glared at her husband. This was his somewhat distant reception to her return. Beth looked at his face in exasperation and shook her head distastefully. How could he be so selfish? She couldn't help herself as she banged the pannier on to the table and blurted out,

"Michal, you don't mean that, your mother is the sweetest thing, look how she helped me to get better. You should be thankful of her and your father too. For putting up with me fretting and worrying over this babe. She was always there when I needed someone to be close. When I felt like my time had come for the Lord to take me. But, how could you know, you were never there!" She dashed towards the cottage door to escape from his onslaught.

He called out after her.

"Mebbe, but remember, you're *mine*, always will be too!" Michal mused, pacing around the kitchen, his chin held in thought by his chapped hand. He flicked a lock of hair away from his eyes with a toss of his head. He was not prepared to be lectured to by a girl, least alone Beth. How dare she try and cross him.

ॐ

Beth stood outside at the edge of the cottage, furious with Michal. She composed herself and was just going back inside when she saw Richard standing on the side of the wood. He glanced back at her briefly then carried on walking. She could see he was upset. She went to follow him but decided against it. She called softly, just so he was able to hear her.

"Richard. I *do* care about you, honest I *do*!"

Richard stopped walking. His back still turned from Beth. His shoulders shuddered with sadness. He continued to walk on down the lane, forgetting that he should have been travelling into Newport. Beth made him forget everything.

❧

Beth watched Richard disappear from sight then returned back indoors, confident she may have just had the edge on her disagreement with her husband. She was fed up with trying to compete with Michal's scornful remarks and his selfish attitude. She looked in his direction and stared him in the eye. Michal drew up a chair.

"Come now, sit you down Beth," he said at length, as he saw her looking anxiously in his direction, trying to anticipate his next move.

"Rest that babe; you need all your strength to give life to him."

❧

Beth didn't reply. She knew when to keep quiet especially as Michal appeared to be in one of his argumentative moods. She could not be bothered with conversation, not now; it would only fuel the disagreement further. Instead she drew the chair up to the hearth and sat carefully down easing herself slowly into the chair, trying to remain in as much comfort as possible on the hard unforgiving surface of the buckled wood that was full of knots and splinters. Her thoughts drifted toward Sullens, of the comforts it bestowed there and the comparison of how different their cottage was. Sullens was cheerful, here was not and never would be. She felt tears welling inside; she tried to put her thoughts far away in her mind. She did long to be with Richard and sooth his grief of the news of the baby. She decided she would have to speak with him soon. She closed her eyes and dozed off to sleep.

~

Beth didn't realise how long she has been sleeping but when she awoke the cottage had slightly transformed for the better. For once Michal had woken up to his responsibilities and was determined to make Beth comfortable, as best he could. He had lit the fire was and the room was warm. He had tried his best to make the tiny cottage cosy, clearing away any scraps of food from the table and sweeping around the fireside. He even made sure the rattrap was out of Beth's watchful eye, he knew she didn't like to see them slain in the cottage in the grotesque handmade wooden trap encased around spokes of rusty wire that Michal had made. The poor rats were subjected to a cruel demise, though Michal was very proud of his invention.

Each day Michal's mother called down with food and fresh baked loaves of bread that she had made in the early morning, to make sure Beth wasn't overdoing things. Beth was ever grateful. She obeyed the doctor's instructions and did not exert herself too much, although sometimes her joy of being pregnant made her feel she was able to do more than she could and her body periodically reminded her when it was time for rest as twinges from inside made her gasp for breath. Beth detested sitting around and was all too keen to continue a normal life.

She was clearly not her normal self and as each day neared its end she became noticeably exhausted. She worried about Richard and how he was feeling. She had not seen or heard from him in weeks. One evening Michal was quite worried at her pale and tired face.

"Come on girl, time for your bed, you look tired," he said sympathetically.

"Don't fuss so Michal. I am all right. I suppose this is what being with child is like. I must get used to this. After all, the baby is not due for a few months yet," Beth sighed and touched her stomach. She felt a tiny kick from within. She gasped making Michal look up in concern. She nodded towards him giving the reassurance he sought that she was fine. When he wasn't looking she winced in pain, biting her lip heavily to prevent the screams exploding from her mouth.

"You'll do as you are told young girl, listen to me, to your bed now," Michal bullied Beth enough to make her slowly rise from her chair by the hearth. Michal steadied her balance by holding her waist from behind. He could be so gentle and understanding these days. Secretly Beth loved the attention Michal was showing her although deep down she knew it wouldn't last forever, so she sensibly made much of it. Leaving her darning behind on the chair and the candle to burn itself out, Beth slowly climbed the stairs. Each step seemed like an endless journey upon a staircase that reached ever skywards. Each step creaked methodically beneath their weight, groaning with every footfall.

∽

Michal had helped Beth to bed and pulled the blankets up close to her face, tucking any remaining edges beneath her body. His mother had kindly leant extra blankets and sheepskins to keep Beth warm at night, as the cottage could be draughty if the wind blew southwesterly. "Got to keep you and the nipper warm ain't we, mustn't let him catch cold now!" said Michal softly.

"You are sure it will be a boy aren't you? Just so he will help you in the wood!" remarked Beth. She felt annoyed that Michal could be so selfish. She hoped for a girl but any sex would make her happy as long as it was healthy.

"What else? He's got to pull his weight when he's older," said Michal seriously as he patted down the covers with an increased force of his large hands causing dust to be blown around the room.

"Poor little beggar," said Beth under her breath.

She felt a wave of slumber overcoming her body as she began to relax. She nestled her head deep into the pillows and closed her eyes waiting to drift off.

"Must have a good strong nipper to help fell all them trees. They don't stop growing and I'll need help when I am an old man that is as long as the Squire wants me to work for him. Who knows, may be I might be Squire one day!"

He stopped talking and lifted his head high, imitating the Squire. He marched around the bedroom in an authoritive fashion, his boots clanking on the bare boards, in a mocking tone he declared.

"*Squire Morey*, can you imagine it, girl? What do you think? How would you like to be married to a.....Beth?"

He looked down and saw the blankets gently moving in time with Beth's methodical and gentle breathing. Her eyes were closed so she obviously was not that bothered over her husband's fantasy of Squiredom.

"No, I couldn't see me as Squire either," he agreed.

With that he picked up the candle and crept downstairs, plunging the bedroom into welcomed darkness. Beth sighed in relief and turned over into a comfortable slumber.

❧

Richard Norris had a chance meeting with Mary Morey earlier that morning, and she told him the news of Beth, knowing full well he would soon spread the news around the village. Richard listened to her and reacted as though he had no idea of the news. He enthused to her about becoming a grandmother and asked how did that make her feel. She responded with a resounding, "Oh I'm truly happy, Richard!" Her face gleaming, she visualised her grandchild-to-be as she clutched her wicker pannier to her broad chest.

"Have they thought of any names yet Mary? Be it a boy I no doubt wonder it will be named after the father, a girl, well after your good self!" Richard could be very charming when he felt the need, if only to glean more information from a slightly gullible Mrs Morey.

"Not as far as I'm sure. Michal thinks it will be a boy. I hope he won't be upset if it isn't."

"Knowing his moods, if it were to be a girl, we'd better keep away from him then, eh Mary!" Richard chuckled but his laughter was short lived.

"Are you telling me Michal is trouble Richard Norris? It seems to me as if you are?" Mary looked him squarely in the eye making him feel quite uncomfortable.

"Heavens no, I'm sorry for making that suggestion Mary, I just thought...."

"Keep your thoughts to yourself, Richard. I must away, to visit Beth. I bid you good day."

"Good day, Mary. Oh, by the way, how is young Beth now?" Richard casually asked.

"She is well, Richard. Why don't you pay her a visit when you're next passing? She would like a visitor, being in that place all day alone."

"Maybe, I'll do that, Mary," said Richard with an awkward smile. He carried on his journey back home. He smiled to himself. He could say the most awkward things sometimes. Diplomacy was not his strongest feature, but he hadn't wished to upset Mary. He just wanted to put his point across about Michal. Mary didn't need to hear that from an outsider, she was only too aware of her son's capabilities. But the invitation to visit Beth was just what he needed.

∽

The following months passed by quickly and Beth began to adjust well to her state of health as she literally bloomed. She had ventured outside for walks on a few occasions and had made it out to the village a few times. Her shape had now noticeably altered from a slim, gangling maiden to a woman on the brink of motherhood, unsure of what lay before her but confident of her intention to become a mother as she sustained an enviable healthy and rosy complexion. All the villagers remarked on her changed appearance, their comments always falling back to how wonderful she looked. Many could not believe it to be the same person, but someone masquerading as her double! Michal, although proud, felt an insane jealousy over all the attention Beth received. To her she was still the same person but bearing his offspring, he could not envisage the fuss that could be made of one with child. Even the local priest had passed the time of day with Michal asking after Beth's welfare and had enquired "How much longer was it until the happy occasion?" Michal hoped it would happen as soon as possible so he could return back to his normal, secluded life and not be bothered by all those busybodies particularly Richard Norris who always knew other people's business often long before they even knew themselves!

❧

Richard stood outside the door of the Morey's cottage. He held a bunch of flowers in one hand and his hat in the other. He was trying to summon the courage to knock upon the door when a voice behind him asked, "Are those for me, Richard?"

He turned to see Beth standing in the lane just coming back from one of her walks she had begun to take upon the doctor's advice. He felt awkward but was able to speak.

"Yes, they're for you, Beth. I hope you like them." He handed them to her. She took them and instantly smelt the aroma they produced.

"They are beautiful, thanking you, Richard. Would you like to come in for a while?" she asked.

"Well, as a matter of fact, Mary said you might like a visitor, so here I am. So, yes I will come in," he replied, bending his hat with anticipation.

Once inside, Beth placed the flowers into a bowl and put them on the table in the kitchen. They instantly brightened the dull room.

"How are you, Beth? Looks like the babe is growing well!" commented Richard looking at Beth's body and the way it had altered.

"I miss you, Richard," she said, moving closer to him. "I miss your touch, your kiss…your…"

Richard moved forward and gently kissed Beth's forehead. She urged his head down to her lips and held them against hers. He didn't resist. He felt that urge of passion rising up inside; a surge that had disappeared since their last encounter. A feeling that he had desperately longed for its return.

"I've missed you too, my love. It's been so long…" he continued to kiss Beth. "I can't stay long; I may be seen by him. You know what he is like, appearing from the shadows."

"It truly is lovely to see you, Richard. Come visit again, won't you?" Beth asked, stroking his hair.

"You can be sure of that, Beth. I'll be away now," Richard grabbed his hat and walked out of the kitchen. Beth stood in the hallway watching him go. She couldn't help feeling that she was falling for this man and this was a feeling that she would have to keep securely to herself because the thoughts of Michal finding out about their liaisons would have a catastrophic effect. Particularly on Richard. She smiled to herself and gently closed the door.

❧

The seasons had begun their automatic mergence from summer to autumn as the luscious green leaves waned and withered to turn to shades of golden and brown and the first early morning frosts of mid-October had started to chill the dawn. Michal had to work on regardless of the weather as the workload began to increase tenfold with the impending, unrelenting winter. The long summer that year had been an added bonus to the woodcutter, giving him extra time to prepare wood supplies, but this certainly would be compensated by the wrath of winter. Beth had spent time during the summer months making him a pair of thick hide trousers with the fleece of a lamb sown inside each leg to overcome the penetrating cold. Michal was a believer that good hard grafting helped to warm the blood and help the circulation to relieve the pain of the biting winter winds. As the weather turned ever colder, the relentless northerly winds raging against his body with each passing day. He returned home with his hands swollen and deeply chapped, blisters on his fingers that were numbed so badly that a good warming by the hearth was needed to bring them back to life. This he always tried to do in secrecy to avoid showing Beth that he was feeling the cold. She might think lesser of him if she saw he was suffering and prone to being, what he would describe, as being weak. He had to remain be the invincible husband who weakened at nothing. Beth never admitted that she saw him on occasions, standing in front of the hearth reaching out to the inviting flames, rubbing life back into his fingers, nursing his hands, feeling out toward the comfort of the blazing logs that crackled periodically, breaking the silence of the cottage. She never wanted to embarrass him or upset him in case his continued good nature of late would suddenly disappear without trace. She felt it best to leave him, his temper would not hold out, diplomacy was her strongest point in their marriage and she thanked God for this gift many times. Michal was always the survivor, always the victor and gave in to nobody or anything. His loyalty was to be admired when many a man would have given in to the cold long previous, but he would continue to battle as long as he could, nothing would get the better of him.

As Christmas time approached, the weather was raging at its cruellest; some said the worst for five years. A fortnight of continuous, relentless rainfall, howling winds, night after night caused the thatch over the cottage bedroom to let in the rain in many places. Drops of water could be heard all over the house and pools laid everywhere places particularly upstairs. During these conditions Michal was worse than a caged, wild animal. That good nature had been tried to the very limits and in his mind he was near to boiling point. He hated the dark nights when the rain was non-stop and he would drag his overcoat on and just walk aimlessly to the end of the lane, to prevent his anger from raging at Beth, particularly as she was so close to giving birth. He would march to the end of Coach Lane to Downend Cross and stride back again as the rain pelted hard into his face like tiny showering pebbles. His huge outline hunched forward against the wild darkening skies, pounding hell bent against the rain and wind. His hair, with rivulets of water cascading down, made his features fiercely sinister as he screwed his mouth into a snarled grimace, trying to prevent the rain and wind from chilling his whole body to the bone, determined to stop the water running down inside his coat. The wind pulled roughly at his coat but he trudged on relentlessly, head bent to the force of the rain back to the cottage against the wind that had reddened his face by exposure to the elements. He did not care, he just needed space and the time to calm himself down and this was the only way he knew to do it. He never met another soul abroad the lane. No one in their right mind would have ventured out on such a terrible night. Many knew Michal's habits of travelling alone at night along the lane, so they thought twice about the chance meeting of an angry woodcutter at dusk. Many were wise to that possibility and would abandon their journeys for another time.

Beth always worried about Michal when he went off into the night like that. She knew his moods were always at their worst during the dark, depressing winter months that seemed to last much longer than their quota for a year. Sometimes, autumn could only last a few days before the onslaught of winter. She had tentatively asked to stay at Sullens on the week leading up to Christmas. It was dry and comfortable there and a little more sheltered and homely than their own cottage. There would also be help and the usual company of relations who also seemed to descend upon Sullens at that time of year.

Michal was not at all pleased about the prospect of having to stay with his parents, still he agreed it would be in Beth's interest to be as comfortable as possible and their own cottage could not offer what Sullens could. Michal's parents were only too pleased to have them stay as Christmas was always a joyful time of year at Sullens, particularly as a new baby was soon to be born into the world. Mrs Morey had remarked that should the baby arrive on Christmas Day it should be named something very special, though she could not quite think what.

Christmas that year brought the coldest weather ever, the rain had turned rapidly to snow and Sullens was soon shrouded beneath a white blanket of drifts over four feet deep. Beth loved the snow and Michal found her like a child gazing out of the window in the parlour one day, "Oh it is so lovely isn't it Michal?"

"It is if you don't have to work in it!" he snarled not even bothering to look at the whiteness outside.

Beth looked at him, her smile disappeared, "I'm sorry Michal, I did not think…"

"Just think… when you speak or don't speak at all!" Michal glared at her, his eyes pierced through her as though she wasn't there.

Startled, Beth walked away from him hoping he would leave it at that and not persist in upsetting her anymore. She knew to leave him alone at these times. She feared one day he may have no hesitation but to strike her where she stood. Lord knows he had threatened it many times in the past but thankfully never gone through with it.

છ

Christmas Eve was spent with members of the Morey family, Michal's older brothers and sisters made their yearly pilgrimage through the snow to the family home for Christmas time. It was always an eventful occasion at Sullens with the grandchildren beyond excitement and the frequent misunderstanding and arguments that always erupted when the family were together. Michal preferred to be out of the lime-light, he would politely acknowledge his family and stay silent most of the time. When he was not working he would sit close to the hearth, chewing his pipe thoughtfully. Christmas Day arrived with a table full of hungry people munching the fare that the women folk had spent an age preparing and which seemed to be lost within minutes devoured amongst a buzz of frenzied chat, laughter and merriment.

After their meal, the men folk descended into the parlour to ponder and digest the past year, to generally talk their affairs to rights and finally to sleep off their fare accompanied by a few more flagons of ale. Whilst the women congregated in the back room with the children playing a few games and gossiping among themselves. "Not long now is it, Beth," remarked Ella, one of Michal's sisters. Beth agreed politely although she was a little tired of this phrase but cleverly hid her annoyance. She looked to the doorway not listening to any of the conversations, wishing Michal would be with her. Instead he lay slumped in the parlour, snoring loudly still clinging to his mug of mead. Only a brave man would attempt to move it from his clasp as he always slept with one eye open as like an animal, ever watchful for its prey.

ↄ

Christmas passed and the winter continued its unfailing onslaught. The snow still laid thick and day after day there was no sign of it melting, the whiteness of the countryside stretched on and on forever. After all the family had left, Beth stayed on at Sullens and Michal returned to work as the demand for firewood was at its height. He had to work all the long, cold daylight hours to keep up. There was no help which made him surly, but being the stubborn man that he was, Michal was determined not to give the Squire the impression that he could not cope with the extra work.

ↄ

A fortnight into January, Beth began to complain of stomach pains and she felt increasingly uncomfortable. Mrs Morey felt she should send for the doctor, so Henry saddled his horse and rode to Arreton, the snow was still quite thick along the lane. On the way he called out to Michal who was working at the edge of the wood amongst a stream of smoke that rose from a fire he had lit earlier that morning to keep warm.

"Michal, son, you had better get back to Sullens, its Beth, I think her time has come for the babe!"

Michal shouted back, "I'll be right there Father, but I'd better get the Squire's word to leave early, what with the extra work he wants me to do. I got to get it done or he'll find another labourer to take me place."

"Don't you worry boy, I'll tell him myself, I've got to go past the Manor, I'll deal with it."

"I'll see you at Sullens," Michal called after his father. He ran back to collect his axe and stamped out the fire with a couple of large kicks of snow from his boots. He hurried as fast as he could though the knee high drifts of snow, his legs ached as he stumbled on to the lane. He cursed the snow; with each footstep he slipped and skidded, leaving blackened footprints from the soot of the fire, along the lane his feet numbed by the cold in his haste to reach Sullens. He hadn't seen Richard Norris in the lane battling to keep on his feet and shielding himself from the wind.

"Keeping busy then, Morey!" Richard called out to him. 'He was certainly in a hurry though,' Richard mused. 'Bounding through those drifts, like a scared rabbit in a chase'. Michal could move a pace when he wanted to, just to keep warm perhaps. It wasn't that much later when the doctor passed by him.

Richard enquired if there was something amiss, but again he didn't receive an acknowledgement. He decided it must be Beth's time for the babe. He watched both men traverse along the lane and decided to follow them himself. If Beth was the centre of all this activity, then he wanted to be a part of it. He wanted to be there for her. As he walked he began to think up an excuse to get past Mary Morey and her probable questioning.

℧

Beth's pains had become more frequent and Mary had prepared hot water in a copper warming pan. An assortment of blankets and rugs were heaped on the floor by the bed. She sat at Beth's side soothing her and wiping her brow as she watched the young girl suffer contractions at an increasing rate.

"All right Beth, breathe deep and try to stay as calm as you can, the doctor will soon be here."

"Is it really happening?" gasped Beth amidst pants of agonised pain. She had broken into a sweat and tried to relax. She gripped hold of the blankets with each burst of pain.

"You are doing fine. Don't you worry your pretty head." Mrs Morey soothed.

"Where's Michal?" asked Beth trying to sit upright. Mrs Morey gently pushed her back down on the bed.

"Henry is calling for him on the way to the village; he should be here by now. Hark I can hear someone at the door at this very time." She called out, "If that is you Michal come straight upstairs!"

"I hear you Mother," came the reply "I am here!"

Michal athletically vaulted up the stairs taking two steps at time leaving snowy footprints all the way. He burst into the bedroom, slamming the door wide open to find his wife lying helpless with an anguished and pained expression on her face. She was wet with perspiration and her complexion was of extreme paleness, hardly a shade of any colour at all. Michal gasped when he saw her.

"Beth, my girl. Are you all right? Have you much pain?" he asked falling to his knees at her side grabbing awkwardly for her tiny hand placing it in his, pulsating it with his every breathe as he fought to regain composure.

"Much pain Michal, but I'm trying to be brave," Beth panted; she gulped as the contractions began once more and this time with more frequency and strength. Beth screamed unashamedly with the pain, it was her own form of momentary relief; the power of her voice seemed to ring around the whole of Arreton valley. Outside in the lane Richard paused as he heard Beth scream. His heart began to pound as he thought of her. He wanted so much to be with her, to share her joy and to support her.

"That's my girl," soothed Michal, his concerned face broke into a smile as he continued holding her hand in his large cold palms, trying somehow to comfort her. His felt excitement and he was totally unaware of the pain she was feeling. His thoughts lay with the unborn child and the anticipation of the imminent birth. He knelt at her side like a wolf ready to capture its prey, his jaw set in a half open gaze, eyes fixed upon Beth's stomach as she writhed on the bed to try to find comfort.

Beth hesitated for a brief moment and turned her head toward Michal, taking in his eagerness; she screwed her face up tight with pain and anger and roared at the top of her voice.

"*God damn you Michal!* God damn you for what you've put me through. You can be blamed for my pain, only you!" She lay back on the bed, tears slowly streamed down her face as she loosened Michal's grip from her hand.

"Leave me be Morey, just leave me," she turned her head away from Michal, her hair sticky from sweat and her tears. She began to sob as she thought of Richard. She murmured so no-one could hear, 'Let me be with Richard.' Mrs Morey gently patted Beth's head with the damp towel, calming her down, whispering soothing words, and at the same time gesturing to Michal to leave the room, without speaking any words. He looked speechlessly at his mother.

"She's delirious!"

Michal got slowly up and stumbled to the landing, amazed at Beth's uncharacteristic outbreak of words cursing him, cursing her husband. There wasn't much that shook the woodcutter, but he was never to forget Beth's words in a hurry.

Soon after, the sounds of a horse and trap muffled by the snow could be heard outside. "The Doctor has come," called Mrs Morey from the landing. "Doctor, please come straight upstairs."

"Hello Mrs Morey, what a day for a babe to arrive, it has started to snow once more; I hope it won't be too thick for my return journey."

"You are welcome to stay if need be, Doctor," said Mrs Morey ushering him into the bedroom.

"You are kind, thanking you," he replied removing his overcoat and hat and bundling them into Mrs Morey's arms who, in turn handed them to Michal who stood motionless in the upstairs landing.

"Michal, take the Doctor's coat downstairs, I think he needs to be alone with Beth now, come on downstairs with you, sit with your father." She urged him away, shoving her son toward the stairs.

Michal grabbed the Doctor's hat and coat and walked towards the door, "See you soon Beth, I'll be downstairs a-waiting."

Mrs Morey gently pulled him away as he quietly protested and disappeared on to the landing. She felt somewhat sorry for Beth's outbreak, something she hardly ever felt for her head- strong son He joined his father in the parlour.

"Did you see the Squire?"

"Yes, I told him what had happened and he expects you back at work later on today, that is if the babe comes today, if not then tomorrow," his father patted Michal on the back in an attempt to reassure him.

After what seemed like hours had passed Michal had become very restless. He had wanted to be with Beth at the birth, but his mother had insisted he stay downstairs, for fear of upsetting Beth further whilst she and the doctor tended to her. He paced up and down in frustration; "You will be no help at all to Beth," his father had told him. He told him to pray for Beth and the baby instead.

The house was unusually quiet until the sweet sound of an infant's first cry rang out at Sullens signifying the birth of a new life. Michal stopped in his tracks and turned his head, "Beth!" he roared and tore upstairs, his father followed at safe distance. Mrs Morey stood at the bedroom door.

"Its all right, come in, and meet your new baby… daughter. Beth's fine but very tired."

Michal rushed into the room and stopped dead staring in awe at the tiny bundle lying in Beth's arms. Beth was exhausted.

"Michal, come see your little girl, look." She whispered, peeling away the blanket from the infant's face. Michal bent down to Beth and laid a kiss upon her perspiring forehead.

"Michal, I'm sorry I tore into you like I did, it was the pain, it was bad, please, will you see it in your heart to forgive me?" Beth laid her hand on top of his, hoping for a response. Michal faintly smiled back at her and slowly closed his eyes, opening them a little afterwards, without speaking she knew he bore no grudge against her.

He gently took hold of the child, gathering up the blanket that was wrapped tightly around her and looked into her eyes. He smiled broadly.

"Hello young lass, welcome to the world, girl!" He looked proudly towards Beth then to his mother, holding the infant high above his head, his large hands clasped gently under her tiny form he declared with a grin on his face,

"I think we should call you Mary, do ya think so, Beth?"

"Yes, I think that would be a lovely name," said Beth smiling a fatigued grin at Michal holding the tiny child, "careful with her, don't you drop her, Michal!"

The Doctor led Mr and Mrs Morey quietly from the bedroom leaving the new family alone.

"Let them be for a while, they need to have some time together." He tactfully advised them, patting Henry Morey on the shoulder.

"Would you care for a little ale doctor, before you go?" asked Mrs Morey in delight. She was flushed with pride. "I cannot believe it; they have named the babe after me!"

As she carried a flagon of ale to the parlour, she caught a glimpse outside of a figure standing in the snow. He was motionless as the snow was beginning to fall more rapidly, covering his black cloak in patches of white. She peered and saw it was Richard. She placed the tray on to a table and knocked on the window, beckoning him to come in. Richard saw Mrs Morey at the window and ran towards the door. She warmly welcomed him in.

"Come on in, Richard. Don't stand out there in that weather. You'll get a fever. Come on, get a mug and have

some of this mead. Beth's just given birth to a little girl…
Mary. It is such a wonderful day!"

Richard smiled at Mrs Morey and her obvious joy.

"I am really pleased for Beth," he replied, taking a
slug of mead. His eyes did not leave the floor.

Mrs Morey continued to pour out mead for her
husband and the doctor. She raised her mug.

"To the babe. To Mary!" she announced. "May God
bless her little soul and welcome her into the world!"

Everyone joined in the toast to the newborn baby.
Richard finished his drink and replaced the mug on the
table.

"I must away, Mary. Before the weather turns worse,"
he announced. "Give Beth my best wishes," he added
without any expression.

❧

Richard slowly walked from Sullens, scuffing the newly
laid snow as he trod. His footprints ached with each step.
The snow had piled higher in the lane and the sky had
turned into a gathering gloom, full of clouds that eluded
a strange yellow tinge. He began on his journey back
to Arreton. His heart was heavy and he felt that he had
lost Beth, not only to a young baby that would demand
all her attention, but to the shameless woodcutter who
didn't deserve such a wife. He sighed as snowflakes clung
to his coat and hat. He began to think about his own life
and how much of a mistake he had made losing Beth.
How he should have had the courage to take her hand

in marriage before she was betrothed to that demon. Richard wondered if there was anyone but he that held so much regret as he did.

CHAPTER FOUR

Little May, as she was affectionately known as, soon became the apple of her Father's ever watchful, protective eye. A beautiful, happy baby blessed with her mother's glossy shock of hair and tender looks soon made Michal forget his thoughts of bringing up a son. Michal was the happiest anyone had ever seen him. Fatherhood was the breath of fresh air he had forever longed for and Beth had been the provider of this newly found happiness.

Richard Norris was walking down Coach Lane when he saw Beth and Little May out in the cottage garden together one day. Beth was holding May and gently cradling her, swaying from side to side. He couldn't resist going up to the gateway and bade them good day.

"Good morning. You have a dear little babe there Beth, well done." He looked across and nodded in acknowledgement to Michal who stood at the doorway and who surprisingly also acknowledged his presence.

Thoughts ran through Richard's mind, he muttered to himself as he continued on his way, "Hope she never possesses her father's temper, what a thing. It could ruin the child." He could not help but notice how pale Beth had looked. He arrived later back at his own cottage only to be greeted by his wife. He mentioned his brief meeting with the Moreys.

"I don't know, through that little smile of hers, she don't seem right at all to me, but I'm no doctor. Perhaps it's the babe giving her plenty of sleepless nights!" Richard announced nonchalantly as he poured out ale into his mug.

"Don't you fret over young Beth Morey," Mrs Norris declared," She be all right, as long as Mary looks after her, don't know about Michal, beyond him, I reckons."

The winter months silently ticked past like a clock that needs winding up but never actually stopping. Time never stood still long enough. The snows had gradually melted away making Michal's working day a little easier for him. On some days, Beth would take Little May up to the wood to show her where her father spent his day. They would often take some food and spend time together before Michal continued toiling until dusk. Little May grew quickly into a very pretty girl and Michal was very proud of her. More winters came and went and Michal and Beth were blessed with three more children, George, the boy Michal had always longed for then, Jacob and baby Luke, who sadly only saw two winters before his untimely death. No one really knew the cause, some said it was fever, others were not convinced; it was never a subject brought up much; particularly in the Morey household; Beth felt she was to blame over losing Luke. However much Mrs Morey tried to reassure her that it was an act of God, Beth unfortunately never got over his death. She blamed herself for being a bad mother and not noticing the signs of his failing health, the constant crying, which she believed the child to be cutting teeth.

She mourned his loss for many years and began to lose interest in life itself and her position of mother to the rest of her children. She had started to shirk her domestic responsibilities. It was something she hated herself for, but be it her mind or her circumstance, she found she could no longer cope with three growing children. She looked towards her daughter, little May, for help. Beth taught her to darn, cook and clean which May thrived on as it made her feel very important and grown-up. Little did she realise her mother's despair as Beth was capable of completely shadowing her true feelings.

May, being the eldest child at the tender age of thirteen was a great help to her mother. She soon learnt how to help care for her younger brothers, how to cook meals and clean the house and how to grow vegetables in their little garden Michal had reluctantly dug over for her. She matured very quickly, helped on by Beth's disposition, taking on the role as a mother herself scolding the youngsters if they misbehaved. She was a credit to her parents and gave Beth a break from the daily chores, taking much of the responsibilities from her as she had admitted to Little May that she had begun to feel unwell of late. Exhaustion again being the cause of her failing health.   Beth always had seemingly frail health, she picked up any illness that was going around, she was vulnerable and her depressed state added to this problem. But somehow this latest ailment felt different than the other times. This time was much worse, though Little May's help did bring some comfort to her.

"Little May, would you mind just taking the little ones out for a time. Go down to Grandmother's, no stopping on the way mind you. I just need some rest, I feel tired today." Beth rubbed her eyes as she spoke to her daughter, Little May didn't spot the tears that Beth shielded with her hand.

"You will be all right then, Mother?" Little May sensed her Mother's fatigue and became instantly concerned, holding her arm as Beth tried in desperation to hide her grief.

"Yes, I just need some sleep," Beth turned away from May's glances.

"By the time you're back I'll have a feed ready for you all. Go on now bundle them off. Grandmother will love to see you."

"I'll see you later Mother, rest well." Little May waved goodbye at the doorway her arms about the little ones shielding them like a ewe to her newborn lambs. Beth could hear her explaining to her siblings where they were going and that Mother needed a rest, amongst squeals of delight she saw them from the kitchen window slowly making their way towards Sullens, each dressed as best she could manage; she always made an effort to cloth her children well. She turned away from the window and wiped away her tears, sighing she slumped onto the one of the chairs. She ached all over and was suffering from lack of sleep. At night the pain was so intense she could hardly breathe. She hadn't told Michal for fear of worrying him. He had enough problems at work keeping up with the Squire's demands and she didn't want Little May worried at her young age. It was not natural for such a bonny girl to be cast upon with timeless worries. Worries that only adults should endeavour to deal with and solve themselves; that is what Beth had told herself. She hadn't even told Mrs Morey of her situation, someone she would normally confide in if she felt fit; somehow Beth knew her illness to be serious. The pain returned making her wince and she held onto her side. This wasn't any old ailment, something that could be treated with a potion... Deep down, Beth knew this was one illness her body could not fend off. Not even a visit from the Doctor would cure this evil. For some reason she knew it was the last she would see of her family, forever, she dearly wanted to see Michal just once more, but the pain would not let her even cross the room without its penetrating dagger that plunged from deep within. She tried to busy herself by shuffling throughout the cottage, trying in vain to put the excruciating stabbing pain in her side to the back of her thoughts, to concentrate on some chores. She couldn't leave the place in such a mess before her children returned back again from their visit to Sullens. It just would not do. Not fair to burden them...

Beth collapsed onto the cold, uneven stone flagged floor in the kitchen, near to the hearth. The pain surged even more and the throbbing in her head pulsated like a hammer,

"Dear God, please help me, take away this suffering," she whispered. The floor felt icy cold against her face and was no comfort as she grew ever weaker. The children would not be back for hours yet. She had so much work to be getting on with including preparing Michal's meal. She tried to focus her thoughts. Her mind turned to Richard Norris. Since she had bore the children, Richard had kept well away from Beth. She thought of his undying love for her. She remembered his tender kisses; of their secret liaisons when Michal was at work. She thought of his kindness and smiled weakly to herself, 'I'll never, ever forget you, Richard. I will always love you...and I think you know that..." She looked towards the ceiling of the cottage and channelled her thoughts of her admirer and hoped that somehow he too was thinking of her at that same time. She lay helplessly crumpled. Perhaps she could just rest, for today, perhaps it wouldn't matter that much, perhaps Michal would take pity on her, leave her be to rest. Not today, of all days. Beth began to pray softly, reciting the Lord's Prayer, missing words that she couldn't or her mind wouldn't let her remember. She prayed for Michal, for her children and finally for herself.

"Please take a pity on me, Lord. Keep my children safe, make them grow into fine people. Bless Michal, don't be hard upon him." She broke off and sighed to herself making the pain react as she breathed, she took a sharp intake of breath. Life was so unbelievably cruel. Cruel to make her unwillingly leave her family. Cruel to bring so much grief to them. To the very last she thought of no one but her family. She didn't hear the person knocking on the door. It was Richard Norris unannounced. He walked into the cottage.

"Beth, are you here? Beth….oh my Lord…" he rushed towards Beth's slumped body.

"Beth, can you hear me? I will get help…just hold on, my love…"

He grabbed a few scraps of cloths and draped them awkwardly across her. Picking up her lifeless body, he ran as fast as he could towards Sullens, reassuring Beth all the way that she would be all right. He called out frantically as he reached the farm.

"Mrs Morey, quick…come quickly…"

Mary Morey heard the shouting and ran to aid him.

"I called past by the cottage, she was…lying on the floor…I think…I think she is still alive…I'll call for the doctor…"

"Take the horse…make haste, Richard…for all you're worth!"

Mary dragged Beth into the parlour, clothes dropped on the floor as she propped her up on a chair. Little May watched from the doorway.

"Mother…what is happening?" She looked shocked with tears in her eyes.

"Your mother isn't well, May…get water… quickly…"

May rushed to the kitchen and retrieved a jug of water and cup. She held it to her mother's unresponsive mouth.

"Here, let's make her more comfortable…did you notice she was unwell this morning, May?"

"No, she looked all right…she wanted us to go to you…so she could get on with her errands…she never said she felt ill…" May watched her mother as the water slipped down either side of her mouth and not down her throat.

"She aint thirsty, Nanna…she aint drinking it…"

Mary Morey didn't give in.

"The doctor will be here soon…May go fetch your father. Now!"

May rushed to the door and ran as fast as she could. She loved her visits to Sullens to see her grandparents. She enjoyed exploring all the fields and meadows, peering into the hedgerows, looking for berries and playing with the livestock there. It provided her with a sense of freedom a youngster needed. This freedom didn't include visiting her father at work alone in the wood, she knew he had a job to do and it didn't seem permissible to interrupt him especially as his temper could so easily be frayed. At an earlier age she had learnt to respect her father and she always kept her distance. However, on this day she had to find her father in haste. She ran down the winding track to the wood, through the long grasses to where she could see him working in the clearing, she called out as loud as she could as she ran, "Father, father, come quickly, its Mother!"

Michal looked up in surprise and demanded.

"Where is she?" he shook his daughter in concern as she stood before him, he tried to get more information. He saw her eyes were filled with tears that were ready to over flow down her pale little face. He saw her evident concern and he grew alarmed.

"At Nanna's house," Little May sobbed. Michal urged her to go on by increasing his grip around her arms, "What, what, tell me!"

Little May continued, trying to talk without choking,

"She told us to go to Grandmother and Pappy's this morning, we been gone all the day, she's just a-laying on the floor, Nanna can't seem to wake her, Father."

Little May froze in horror as her father loomed large over her quaking body. He scooped her deftly up in his arms and rushed back up the lane to the cottage.

"Where are your brothers? What have you done with them?" Michal gasped as he ran with Mary in his arms, her body joggled along as he made haste.

"They are with Nanna," she cried in despair at her father's urgency. She couldn't understand why he was fretting so much. When they reached Sullens they saw the children on the front door steps with Mrs Morey.

"Michal, I am so very sorry. I have some terrible news. Beth…she is…dead… she died a few moments ago…"

Michal looked towards the open front door. The doctor strode quickly to the house.

"Let me through, Michal…" he urged and pushed past the woodcutter who stood dazed. "Will you all stay here, please?" The doctor ordered.

He returned to the party of stunned members of the family with his hat in his hands.

"I am very sorry, you're right, Mrs Morey. Beth has died, God rest her soul. Heaven knows why she did not come to me for help. For one to suffer in silence shows she was a very brave but foolish girl, right to the end, her concern it seems was only for you and your children. I can only think she did not want you to worry over her, she must have wanted to continue on without fuss. Michal, do you understand what I've just said to you?"

The doctor was alarmed as Michal pushed past him and walked into the parlour, completely transfixed on Beth's dead body, lying awkwardly on the floor beneath a blanket.

Michal stood in shock, his mouth opening and closing with no words coming out, trying to take in what the doctor was telling him. Finally he found his voice.

"I did not know she was so close to death, she never told me. But, Beth was never a fool. Don't let me ever hear you say that again, Doctor," He quivered, running his hands simultaneously through his hair.

"How could she not tell me, how could she. My poor girl, laying there no life in her, God rest her soul, she died and no one to comfort her last breath."

"She would never have told you Michal, she never wanted you to worry, but I believe she never really recovered from her last pregnancy. It seemed to sap all her strength and her energy and what with the baby dying, part of her died, I sadly think, died with him." The doctor picked up his bag, he placed his hand softly on Michal's arm and announced.

"I will leave now, I am so very sorry, my prayers are with you Michal and your family."

The doctor placed his hat on his bowed head and walked solemnly down the path to the lane. Michal watched him go staring in disbelief; tears began to well in his eyes as he looked to the sky and yelled in uncontrollable anger.

"How could you do this to me? To the children! To Beth! What sort of God are you? Why do you always treat me so badly?" He started to walk away from the cottage. He glimpsed the Doctor's carriage disappearing up the lane towards Arreton. Little May ran after him.

"Father! Father! I love you, Mother has gone. You still have me, Father! Father!" she cried in her bravest voice, tears streaked her pretty face.

Little May stopped as she saw Michal disappear far from view. Henry comforted his wife as they stood in despair in the kitchen. They were surrounded by the rest of the children looking bewildered at each other, not making a sound.

"What are we to do now?" Mrs Morey asked, her voice was distant. "What is to be of the children?"

"Take the children to the kitchen, I'll go to the Parson, get him to give a blessing in this house. I'll call into the church and arrange for Beth's body to be taken away as soon as they can." Henry Morey ushered the children from the kitchen, pushing his wife to leave as well.

"We can't just leave her like this Henry, what..." Mary Morey despaired.

"Leave it to me; Michal won't be back for an age, I'll deal with this affair."

Sadness and grief had arrived at Sullens that year.

❧

Richard Norris was informed by the doctor, later that day of Beth's death. When told he sat quietly in his cottage, staring at the ground. His eyes were filled with salty tears that slowly dripped across his cheeks. He was inconsolable and felt guilty that he had neglected to visit Beth before she died. He, like everyone else was terribly shocked over the sudden demise of such a beautiful, loving woman.

Richard felt a strong urge to tell Michal of his love for Beth and he was overcome by a sudden anger that Michal was probably to blame for her death. For the way he treated Beth, how she slaved relentlessly over him.

He decided to visit Sullens the next day and found Mrs Morey at home. She answered the door, dressed in black.

"Oh, Richard. Come in, please," she welcomed him, with tears in her eyes.

"Mary, I just wanted to say…that…" Richard couldn't hold his feelings and was so choked that he couldn't speak. Mrs Morey put her arm around his shoulder.

"Come now, Richard. Please don't fret. We *all* loved her so much…thank you for finding her when you did… she would have died alone if you hadn't called upon her, take comfort in that thought…" Mrs Morey soothed and stroked Richard's head that was bent to the floor, trying to hide his tears.

Somehow, Mrs Morey had always known that Richard was very fond of Beth. She had seen the signs but had never uttered a word to anyone.

"Come now, my lad. She's free from pain and suffering now. I know that…and I know that she wouldn't want you to grieve. Remember her and her life. Remember just how pretty she was. And, like us, I know you'll always love her."

Richard wiped away his tears and managed to acknowledge Mrs Morey's words. He felt surprised at this statement but smiled and gently kissed her hand, as a form of gratitude.

"Thank you, Mary. Thank you for your words. But how did you know about my feelings for Beth?"

Mrs Morey smiled. "Let's just say, instinct, Richard. But worry not. I'll never breathe word to a soul. It'll be our secret, all right?"

Richard sighed heavily and composed himself.

"If you need me, you know I'll only be too happy to help you."

"Thank you, Richard. We've got to get through tomorrow, the funeral. The Lord knows it will be so hard. I know you want to be there. Please come...you will won't you?"

"I'll be there, Mary," Richard replied. He placed his hat slowly back on to his head.

Mrs Morey watched as Richard walked slowly away from Sullens. She sighed to herself and found her own grief return once more. She thought of Michal and the children and gently wiped away her own tears.

Beth's funeral was held the following morning at St George's Church in Arreton village. Michal was hardly able to contain his grief, but he felt no one should see him break down not even his grief stricken children, so he hid his own grief as only he knew how by forcing it to the back of his mind. He distantly heard the service and the sermon preached by the Parson, although the words spoken meant nothing to him. His eyes were transfixed towards the downs in the far off distance. He could see the clouds lying close to them; giving the impression the sky was very low that day. A flock of birds flew by overhead and Michal wished that Beth might be one of them, flying to her freedom, with no worries or cares to burden her voyage. He longed to see her, hoping he could pick her face out from the array of clouds that scudded across the bleak skies. His distraction returned to the burial service, of how wonderful Beth had been and what a tragedy to be struck down at such a young age and, as he stood by the grave side, he watched the coffin lowered awkwardly into the cold ground to the sound of the sombre death knell that pealed with each movement of the ropes that encapsulated the coffin. He tightly clutched a few flowers in one hand and his hat in the other. Throwing the bunch aimlessly into the grave amidst clods of earth, it fell neatly onto the coffin's surface and he bade his silent and final farewell to dear Beth.

Richard stood a little distance away from the graveside, behind the Morey family. He was accompanied by his wife who spent much of the time consoling members of the congregation. He looked toward Michal and focussed on the woodcutter's grief. 'If only you knew how I felt about your wife, how I loved her, even more that *you* did. I could have made her happier. I could have helped her live. I would've looked after her. More than you *ever* would. May you rot, Morey. Rot in *hell*.' He felt his shoulders squaring up as his words remained tightly held within his own mind. He longed to spill them in unrelenting fury to the woodcutter. As he stood at the graveside, Richard vowed one day that he would get even with Michal. No matter what it took, his revenge would be sweet.

The cortege of family and friends drifted away from the churchyard as the gravediggers were left to continue their task to cover the coffin with the freshly dug earth; enclosing the body of Beth forever. Richard waited until the family were out of sight then returned to the grave and placed a bunch of three, sweet-smelling yellow roses on it.

"These are for you, my love. To show how much I truly loved you. May God always look after you and guide you to the better life."

He took one last look at the grave and walked silently away.

❧

Later, that same year, Henry Morey passed peacefully away at Sullens and Michal realised that his fight against tragedy seemed to be waning. He despised the fact that God was taking his family one by one away from him, controlling each person's life as he felt fit, made him so very bitter. He spent much of his time alone. Not only did he still grieve for his beloved Beth, but now also his father whom he had adored and who had left his mother to cope alone with the children. She had worshipped her husband and for him to leave her so suddenly, left a large, gaping hole in her fraught and tired life. Mrs Morey had decided it would be best for the children to spend as much time as possible at Sullens to enable Michal to continue working. It was also the chance for her to be kept preoccupied taking her mind off her grief. Little May, who had reached her mid-teenage years, worked hard helping her father. Michal had not realised just how much help Little May was to him until after Beth's death.

One day she approached him in the cottage. Walking up to him she tentatively announced, "Father, I have found work. I have found a good employer; I start in two days time."

Michal stared at his daughter. He could see Beth in her eyes. He was surprised at her announcement. He hoped she would stay working for him, but didn't condone it. He replied smiling at her anxious face,

"That is good, well done girl," he appeared to be genuinely pleased for her. "So where is this work then girl, Newport? Arreton? Who will you work for?"

He quite expected her to say just down the road, labouring at one of the farms.

"Father, it is at Freshwater. For the Squire there."

She awaited the response hardly daring to breathe. Quite expecting her Father to explode into a lecture of where her responsibilities lay, but unpredictably he didn't. Instead he became worryingly quiet and replied in a silent whisper.

"Oh… I see," Michal looked a little taken aback. He regained his smile. "That is fine Little May, just fine. Don't fret about us, your grandmother will manage, we will be all right, even though you will be twenty miles distant."

"So you will give me your blessing then?" asked Little May desperate to please her father. She twisted a piece of grey material from her skirts in her fingers, holding it tightly in anticipation. Eventually he spoke, after much thought, a trait that had appeared in him since the loss of Beth.

"What man would not give his own daughter his blessing?" said Michal as Little May ran towards him and flung her arms around him, half laughing, half crying, she hugged him back in part relief, in part gratitude.

"Go forth girl, work hard and prosper, you deserve to do well! Earn yourself a living. Get out from this cursed valley. Meet new folk."

છ૭

Little May was so relieved. She had been worried about her father's reaction to her news ever since she had been offered the work. She had come to hear of it through one of the girls in the village, that the Squire at Freshwater was looking for servants. Freshwater was a long way off; a good day's travel by coach and four and she would not be able to come home very often. Michal hugged his daughter back, holding her tightly in his muscular arms, but he couldn't help feeling he was losing another part of Beth, though he never showed his emotions, he wouldn't spoil Little May's chance for success. He hoped that her life would be a better and more successful one than his own.

☙

The day little May left the cottage was a sad day for Michal. She was young but she was as mature as her dear mother had been. She had grown up so rapidly that it worried Michal that she had missed out in some way on her brief childhood. Little May now stood before her father clutching a small leather pannier and her wicker basket. She kissed him gently on the cheek.

"God bless you Father, I will try to visit soon, goodbye."

Michal hugged her in return.

"God bless you as well Little May Morey, your mother would be proud of you. Who knows, she's probably looking down on you now!"

He watched her as she began her walk towards Newport to meet the stagecoach. Her flaxen coloured hair flowing loose in the wind and her petit frame trod in determination to make a living for herself. Staring up into the clouds, he sought Beth's visage again.

"Look at her, Beth," he murmured, "Look at Little May. She's leaving home. Keep yer eyes upon her, guide her."

He smiled to himself and walked up the pathway to the cottage as her outline against the lane gradually became difficult to see. Freshwater beckoned and the chance of suitable work with a new life as well. As she disappeared from his view Michal realised he had just witnessed Little May's transformation from a child to a young woman. He stood for a while and felt the welling of his long awaited tears.

CHAPTER FIVE

Little May's journey to Freshwater had been very long and arduous. The coach hadn't been very comfortable at all. The road held many hidden holes and the coach wheels seemed to find all of them, making her whole body judder and leave her seat on countless occasions. There were two other people travelling with her. One, an elderly woman who kept asking Little May if she was all right and that she was so young to be travelling alone. The other was a man who never uttered a word but kept himself engrossed in a book, which periodically leapt out of his hands when the coach hit a particularly large hole. Little May laughed to herself each time this happened, but the man just picked up his book and silently continued to read as though nothing had happened. The coach eventually arrived at Freshwater just as the sun was beginning to set. Little May found herself stepping from the coach and staring first at the coach horses that were hot and tired, their large bodies steamed with sweat as the groom led them away to the nearby mews to rest for the night after their long haul, and then at the large house that was to be her place of work and also more importantly to Little May, her new home. She straightened her shoulders and stretched her aching body and walked nervously towards the front door, clutching her bags that contained a few items of clothing and a loaf of bread that she hadn't touched. Just as she raised her hand to knock, a voice behind made her start with fright.

"Don't knock the front door girl! You must be the new servant, come over here, through this way! Don't *ever* go to the front, that aint for servants, just them and the Squire."

Bewildered, Little May turned to where the shrill and impatient female voice had emerged, as she did so the voice rang out again.

"Here girl, are you blind? Over *here*!"

Little May glanced towards a rotund woman with a large red face with puffed out cheeks, who was stood at a side door, wearing a large flowing apron over a brown dress. She was gesturing to Little May in an authoritative fashion, her raised, chubby hand impatiently beckoned her to make haste and approach in that direction. Little May guessed she must be the head cook whom she was to report to. She reached the side door.

"Hello, I am May Morey, the new servant." She announced, curtseying at the same time, trying to make a good impression.

"I thought as much, now come in girl, I can't stand here all day waiting for you. I am Mrs Amos, the head cook. You are to start work with me in the kitchen. You will report to me each morning at half past five, don't be late mind you; I can't bear sloppy servants who can't manage their time keeping. Make sure you get that hair tied back, no flowing locks allowed, not in my kitchen!"

Little May decided there and then that Mrs Amos was not a person to be crossed. She reminded her of her father with her tone and no nonsense manner. Little May felt an air of respect must be paid to this lady as much as possible. As she began to take off her bonnet and cloak, Mrs Amos said,

"Now then, I'll get Susanna, one of the other maids to show you to your room, you can unpack and afterwards get started in the kitchen. Have you eaten today?" asked Mrs Amos fussing around Mary, looking at her clothes and trying to assess her capabilities as her new assistant.

"Not since this morning," replied Little May. "I was too nervous to eat anything, I couldn't."

"Then I will find you some food tonight but, for future, you must cook your own. I'm not here to wait on you young lady!"

"Yes, Mrs Amos," said Little Mary wearily. The journey had made her very tired and she could hardly stand up. Her legs felt like they were made of lead weights and her bags made her arm ache and whatever Mrs Amos was saying was not really making a great impression on Little May, not at this late hour.

She was escorted up several small, winding staircases and shown to her room at the very top of the house by Susanna the other maid that Mrs Amos had mentioned.

"Hope you like it here, May" she said, "Don't let Mrs Amos upset you too much. She means well."

"Thanking you Susanna," said Little May gratefully. She walked into the room where she was to sleep. It was sparse but cosy with a bed in the corner under the sloping roof and a small table with a washbasin and jug sat upon it. A single wooden pole was her wardrobe and, at the far end of the room, was a tiny window. Mary walked across and looked out into the half-light. The window had a good view across the roof to the pretty gardens below. Placing her bag onto the bed Little May had a feeling that she would enjoy her time here.

A few weeks had passed by and Little May had settled in very well. She adored being amongst so many busy people, all with their own daily tasks to carry out. She was able to keep to her routine and always ensured she was never late reporting to the kitchen in the early hours of each morning. Living and working at the Squire's house gave her a large sense of security, all the other servants were very helpful and kind to her, that is all except Mrs Amos!

Being the new girl, Little May was constantly targeted by the large cook, who made sure it was drummed into her head that she was the youngest, the smallest and had the most to learn. If anything went wrong it was always Little May's fault, even if she was not in the kitchen at the time, she always accepted the blame fearing Mrs Amos and never daring to cross her.

One afternoon as she was arranging the contents of a kitchen cupboard she heard, the familiar voice

"For the Lord's sake May, hurry up and tidy that cupboard out! You've been day dreaming my girl. I have lots of other jobs for you today when you've finished that. There are pheasants to be plucked and dressed as the Master has a dinner party tonight and twenty guests arriving, now hurry up!" boomed Mrs Amos.

"Yes, Mrs Amos," said Little May in despair. Although she was now getting used to Mrs Amos' manner, she was concerned by the cook's attitude towards her. She decided it would be best to keep out of her way as much as possible to avoid any potential unpleasant scenes, as sometimes Little May felt her own temper would begin to rise to challenge the cook and that would never do. She thought of her old home, of her father labouring away in the wood, his chapped hands and overworked body bent over trunks of felled timber, of her brothers and sister and she felt tears being to prick her eyes.

"May! May! Where are you?" yelled Mrs Amos "Get started upon those birds before their bodies rot under their feathers!"

"Yes, I'll start them straight away!" yelled back Little May. As Mrs Amos turned her back, May started to imitate the bellowing cook by wagging her finger in the air with her other hand on her hip. She said "I've told you time and time again about being lazy!" under her breath so no one could hear.

❧

As May turned she suddenly felt a stinging sensation on the back of her head as Cook's hand caught her unmistakably and painfully like a bolt of lightning.

"May! Get to work!" she screamed at the young girl.

Fearing her mockery of Mrs Amos had been discovered, she ran out of the kitchen door to the outhouse and picked up two pheasants at once on to her lap and began frantically plucking the birds simultaneously with both hands. Feathers flew in all directions as the pheasants became the brunt of Little May's anger.

"I hate you! I hate you!" she hissed, determined to seek revenge somehow on Mrs Amos.

Little May gasped aloud.

"Why does she hate me so much? What have I done?" Her eyes became red and swelled with her tears. She wiped them away on the sleeve of her arm and sniffed. She was determined not to let the cook upset her any further.

Later that afternoon, twelve plucked and beautifully dressed pheasants lay on the kitchen table ready to be cooked. As Little May was tidying up the spent feathers that were scattered everywhere in the outhouse, a voice suddenly spoke behind her and remarked,

"You have quite enough feathers to stuff a mattress here!"

Little May turned round in surprise to see a young man standing in the doorway. He looked to be in his early twenties with fair hair and warm green eyes; he was very well dressed and spoke in soft and gentle voice. He walked towards Little May raising his hat.

"Hello, my name is Thomas Dove, I was just passing by when I noticed all these feathers and I wondered, pray from where they were coming?"

Little May immediately curtsied, acknowledging his presence.

"Yes sir, it is a bit of a mess I'm afraid, I dare not stop or Cook will have another excuse to shout at me again. I will tidy it away now sir, right away."

"Is she really as bad as I am led to believe?" enquired Thomas.

"She likes to think she can scare me, but I never let her win, sir," sighed Little May. "Sometimes," she added, "she upsets me more than she will ever know sir. The problem is I am the youngest, the new girl and most… I'm easy pickings for her, she has a nasty streak and I think deep down that she is the devil disguised as a cook and one day she will burst into fire and die a horrible death!"

"Strong words for such a pretty girl," said Thomas, smiling at the young maid's outburst. "I am impressed by your feisty determination!"

"I am told it is from my mother, she is dead, God rest her soul sir," said Little May looking directly to the floor, avoiding his face assessing the scores of feathers yet to be collected up.

"I am sorry," said Thomas "But somehow you must have inherited her good looks as well, in that case." He stood with his hands clenched behind his back beneath his coat tails, looking to Little May's face.

Little May shyly turned away. She felt her face turn scarlet. She started to sweep the rest of the feathers that blew about in circles above the ground with her continual furious brushing.

"I must be away," said Thomas "I have a meeting to attend this afternoon in the village. I am pleased to have made your acquaintance uh, I am sorry but you have not told me your name."

"Oh, my name is Little May… May Morey, Sir."

"I am pleased to have made you acquaintance Little May Morey," Thomas continued. "Perhaps, one day we shall meet again?"

Little May smiled quickly and curtsied, awkwardly this time.

"Yes sir, perhaps."

She watched him walk across the courtyard to a waiting carriage. He walked with an elegant air and she was suitably impressed by his kindness.

"Perhaps we *will* meet again, I hope so kind sir," whispered Little May, staring after Thomas Dove. She leant on her broom as she heard her name being shrieked out by Mrs Amos. Little May had lost count how many times that day. She muttered under her breath,

"I am here you cursed old hag!" Then aloud; "Coming, Mrs Amos!"

Little May wondered what life was like back home in Arreton. At times she felt homesick but the nature of her employment kept her busy all day. In fact, it was nearing nightfall at Sullens. The winter days were very short now with the light hours quickly dispersing into night fall around four o'clock in the afternoon.

Michal was returning slowly home along Coach Lane. He could see the twinkling lights of Sullens against the winter sky. It had been a dull, cold day no sunlight to speak of and it made him feel depressed. Since Beth had died, Michal had moved in permanently to Sullens with his children. His mother ably brought them up and Michal was indebted to her help. It was close on two years since Beth had died and there had not been a day go by that Michal didn't pine for her comfort and love. The loss too of his father bought sad memories to Sullens at this time of year. He thought of Little May, of having to say goodbye to his dear daughter now so long ago, he felt that nothing could ever go right for him again. He had suffered his share of grief and the torment from the ghosts within his mind. At night as he tried to sleep but visions of Beth turned over and over in his mind he could plainly see her pretty face smiling and waving to him. She always asked him the same, enquiring question.

"Michal, come join me, I love you. I miss you. Please Michal, join me now!"

Many nights, he awoke with a start to find his entire body drenched with sweat and shaking uncontrollably. His visions of Beth were almost real. He called out her name many times and often had woken his mother who was lying in the next room. She would open her son's bedroom door and peer at him only to find him lying in the darkness asleep. In case he was awake, she would softly call out, "God bless you Michal." She would then return to her own room with tears in her eyes. She prayed to God for hope and strength as her thoughts turned to her beloved Henry, a husband so strong and loving taken from her when she needed him the most. She returned then to her own troubled slumbers.

ᔅ

The following day Little May was still thinking of home when she saw from the scullery window, Thomas Dove climb down from a carriage that had just pulled up in the drive. It looked like he had a delivery to make as he held a prettily wrapped parcel in his hand. Little May straightened her cap and brushed her dress down quickly with her hand. She straightening the creases on her apron and removed any unsuspecting dust and cobwebs as she had been clearing the cellar that morning and hoped she hadn't made herself too dirty. Her breath caused a mist upon the window obscuring her view, as she saw Thomas stride to the front door and knock upon it.

"May, where are you, come help me fill these pies!" came the inevitable yell from Mrs Amos.

"Yes, Mrs Amos!" Little May, this time in absolute delight skipped into the kitchen, her face glowing.

"What has gotten into you girl? Why, you look quite flushed! Have you got a fever?"

"Do I look flushed?" exclaimed Little May "Do I really? I feel quite alive! But no fever, Mrs Amos!" she cooed to the cook, leaping energetically around the kitchen, lifting her skirts as though she was about to dance.

"Less of your nonsense May Morey, come on there is work to be done. Get these rabbits gutted in haste and prepare that salt ham over there on the table."

Mrs Amos began fussing around in the kitchen, poring over the freshly baked pies that sat steaming giving the kitchen a wonderfully enticing aroma. She was finally beginning to warm to Little May. It had taken well over two years, but now Little May had grown into quite a young lady. The cook was secretly impressed with the way Little May was adapting to work but she never could bring herself to praise the young girl. It would be beneath her own personal standards and in any case, she did not want the girl to rise above her station as scullery maid. That would never do and she despised the thoughts of someone younger being able to take on her role as cook. No, Mrs Amos vowed to herself, the girl was adequate and she should be kept firmly in her place, never to be given the chance of a free rein.

જી

There was a commotion coming from the hall.

"Where is the scullery maid? May are you there? There is a Mr Thomas Dove to see you!"

Little May could hardly believe her ears, not only had she the pleasure of seeing Thomas again, but he actually wanted to see her! She felt shocked that he has asked to see her and she felt a twinge of panic.

"Can I go Mrs Amos? I have someone to see me," asked little May, hardly able to hide her joy.

"So… I see," said Mrs Amos frowning in bewilderment and wondering why on earth the young man wanted to associate with a servant. She looked towards Little May, scanning her appearance with a critical eye.

"At least wash your face and hands before you go and don't wait around. Be straight back mind you, I have no spare time at all today, let alone you talking to a gentleman. Heaven only knows why he wants to speak with you, could be for plucking him some pheasants maybe, anyway be off and be back here straight away."

"Yes, Mrs Amos, I'll be back soon, don't you worry, I'll work hard!" called out Little May as she ran into the hall.

She passed by a looking glass and caught her reflection, her face looked clean; she quickly rubbed the end of her apron over her face to make quite sure there were no stray cobwebs from the cellar. She found Thomas standing at the far end of the hall, his hat held in one hand and the other carrying a package. Mary slowed her pace and tried to walk calmly toward him. She felt her heart rush suddenly which made her gasp.

"Good morning Little May Morey, how have you been?" asked Thomas smiling at her.

"I fair well sir, thanking you for asking. What brings you here, sir? " she asked in awe, her eyes bright and excited forgetting to curtsey.

"I have a gift for you, I was passing so I thought I would drop by," Thomas answered and handed her the package.

"A gift! For me? No one has ever bought me a gift except my grandmother at Christmas, that was two years ago!" declared Little May.

"Well, are you not going to look at what I have brought for you?" Thomas asked.

"What is it?" asked Little May in wonder as she tore at the crimson ribbon that held the secret.

"Open it and you will soon find out," coaxed Thomas, charmed by her innocence and genuine surprise.

Wiping her hands rapidly on her apron to make sure her hands were clean, Little May undid the ribbon letting it fall to the ground and gasped in surprise at the brightly coloured silk shawl that lay inside.

"Oh it is so lovely, but why for me?" she asked in surprise, "It is so lovely, thank you so very much, sir!"

"I bought it because I wanted to buy you something pretty for you to wear. I bought it because I would like you to wear it when I take you for a drive into the countryside the weekend next," replied Thomas solemnly, awaiting her response to his proposition.

"Oh my lord, but I never have time off," exclaimed Little May, shocked by his announcement.

"I will see to it that you will next weekend. I will speak with *your* Mrs Amos, don't fret, May."

"Thank you very much sir, you are too kind to me. I must go now or cook will start her shouting again."

"Until next Sunday, at noon then," said Thomas.

"Yes, goodbye sir, thanking you again!" called Mary and she dashed back to the kitchen, forgetting her manners she stopped and curtsied at the doorway muttering her apology and feeling her cheeks flare up in embarrassment.

෴

From that day Little May was floating on air, she was so overwhelmed by her visitor that she could not concentrate on her work so cook decided to give her a few hours away from work to calm down. Little May dashed up the narrow stairs to her room in the attic and wrapped her shawl around her shoulders, she sat upon her bed in sheer disbelief, she breathed in the newness of the material and the faint fragrance of Thomas Dove.

"Mr Thomas Dove is taking me on a carriage ride. Mr Thomas Dove is taking me out! Mr Thomas… oh dear Mr Thomas! I shall not sleep until next Sunday but I must! I must try!" She swooned.

Her heart began to pound in anticipation. She got up and walked to her window and peered beyond the gardens to open fields beyond and imagined herself riding on a black stallion with Thomas. He held her firmly round the waist and whispered into her ear as they cantered through endless meadows of buttercups in hazy sunshine, a golden hue engulfed Thomas' face like an angel. Her dream was interrupted by someone outside on the landing. She distantly heard a voice calling her name.

"May, are you in there? Will you come out?"

"Yes...who is it?" called Little May in a dreamy stupor, her eyes fixed on the view outside as she relived her fantasy.

"May, you *know* who I am, open the door, now!" The voice insisted.

Little May walked toward the door, her shawl still draped unevenly around her shoulders covering her clothes. She called out, "Who are you?" in uncertainty. She felt the voice was vaguely familiar, yet so distinct. Again it called to her.

"Come and join me outside, you will love it, it is so beautiful here!"

Little May slowly opened the door and walked out onto the landing, "Hello, whose there?" she called again.

Now there was only silence. Little May became slightly uneasy, she swore she heard a voice calling her name, it must have been her imagination but she was almost sure it was the voice of her dear mother. "I must have been dreaming," she concluded, feeling a little puzzled, she walked back into her room and, as she closed the door Little May failed to observe the shadowy, grey figure slowly disperse into the air at the far end of the landing.

At last Sunday had finally arrived much to Little May's huge relief. The week had seemed like a decade to her with each day dragging slowly into the next. Thomas Dove had arranged for her to have the afternoon off by plying Mrs Amos with a gift of flowers arranged into a pretty posy.

At noon Little May heard the hooves of horses and wheels of a carriage drawing up into the gravel drive. She dashed immediately toward him; her shawl carefully arranged round her shoulders and curtsied. Thomas met her half way across the courtyard and escorted her to the carriage. He helped her climb up inside the team of black shimmering cobs impatiently pawed the ground. Little May was so taken aback by the carriage and for the fact that Thomas was able to employ a driver for that afternoon. She sat quietly gazing out through the carriage window.

Mrs Amos had continually drummed into her that morning to always remember to call him 'sir' and to remember her manners at all times and not to speak out of term. Little May was also advised by the fussing cook to wear her Sunday best and try to look as presentable as she could. Little May's choice of clothes were few so she tried her best to impress her suitor, hoping he wouldn't see the patches on her skirts where she had darned them to prevent the fraying edges from tearing further.

As the carriage and horses drove from the house Thomas was smiling. He was enchanted by the way Little May sat like a statue silently gazing out the window as they made their way into the countryside. Little May breathed in all the familiar scents from the surrounding countryside, dog rose, elder and bramble. It was a bright but brisk afternoon and the wind against her face was so refreshing yet numbing. Little May was glad she had the shawl to keep her warm.

"I do not need to ask whether you are enjoying your trip." Thomas spoke eventually.

"Yes I am sir, I truly am, sir…thank you…sir," said Little May beaming at her host.

"Pray, why do you call me sir?" Thomas asked in surprise.

"Because Mrs Amos… um, thought it would be best," said Little May. "You being a gentleman and all…" She felt embarrassed and looked to the floor of the carriage.

"Oh, so *cook* put you up to it did she now?" asked Thomas in wonder.

"Yes, she said I should call you sir. But anyone of importance I call sir, sir," said Little May.

"Well, I say you call me Thomas and nothing else," he reassured her by lightly touching her hand simultaneously as he spoke. It felt warm and comforting, Little May warmed to his touch, his hand was so smooth.

She turned away as could feel her heart begin to race. Thomas took her hand in his.

"May, I find you deeply attractive and I hope you will enjoy being in my company this afternoon. I have arranged for you to dine at my house. Please say you will stay and dine with me?"

Little May looked at him and smiled noticing how eager he awaited her reply she said,

"Thank you…I would love to, er…Thomas!"

He squeezed her hand tightly; he could not hide his pleasure, "I am *so* glad."

Thomas lived just a few miles away at Brook in a rambling house that overlooked the sea. May had never seen the sea before and was amazed how romantic it was. Such a perfect location, a place she could not even have even dreamed about, serene, peaceful with an air of vague extravagance, not that she was aware of such a life. He father had spoken of the wealthy folk, but she never thought she might be given the opportunity to experience this life. Dinner had already been prepared by his housekeeper in the dining room and it was the best food Little May had ever tasted. After lunch Thomas took her into the gardens. As they strolled around May stopped to take in the view, "You have a beautiful home and just look at the sea, it is so lovely. I could spend hours just looking." She felt honoured to be walking in with him in such a beautiful location.

"Yes, I enjoy living here May, but it sometimes feels a lonely place, one man, occupying a house with no one to share it with me. It can be miserable."

"My family all live at Sullens in the country near to Newport. There is my grandmother, my father and my brothers who all live together. I miss them all. Do you know, I thought I heard my mother calling me two days passed at the house, I was in my room but when I went to find her, there was no one there…"

"Sweet May, the imagination plays cruel tricks on one's mind sometimes," said Thomas.

They continued to walk around the garden when Thomas suddenly stopped. He turned to May taking hold of both her hands he said,

"May, when I first saw you, I felt a great affection for you. I have never felt that sensation before, but I now know that you mean a great deal to me. Since first I saw you with all those feathers, I have thought of nothing but you. I hope I am not making you feel uncomfortable? But I want you to know how I feel about you." He paused, a sense of relief flooded from him as he realised he was actually saying what he had been bottling up.

May grinned shyly at him. She looked at him as his eyes focused on the ground. She felt his embarrassment as she remained silent. She noticed that he had increased his grip on her hands and how his palms had beads of perspiration as they lay moist upon her fingers.

"Thomas," May spoke clearly and staring at him announced, "I have felt that same thing as well, something I have never known before. I could not hardly wait until this day. I have a warm feeling in my heart; I think it could be the feelings of affection...love."

Thomas looked into her sky blue eyes.

"May, I think I am in love with you." He leant towards her and kissed her gently on the lips at first in uncertainty and then once more with passion that flowed through his veins like never before.

May adored the soft touch of his face and lips against hers, she loved the smell of him, his complexion and his passion surging inside like a volcanic eruption that was waiting to cascade from him. She felt him take hold of her waist and hold her tightly against his body. They stood alone hugging one another for what seemed like an age surrounded by a beautiful garden and listening to the sound of waves crashing on the rocky beach below.

"May, you are more beautiful than I first remember, more than I could ever imagine. I can not believe my fortune," Thomas sighed as he hugged her.

"I too, feel the same," said May. "I am so lucky to have met you, Thomas. What news I will have to tell my family! They won't believe me. You will have to come and visit them one day, to meet them!"

"There is nothing I would like better, May. In fact there is nothing I would like more than to see you whenever I can."

They began to walk back to the cottage through the array of trees and shrubs in the garden.

"I must be getting back soon, I have work to do," said May.

The afternoon had passed by too quickly.

"I will get you back to Freshwater soon, but you must promise me that we will meet again next Sunday."

"Nothing will stop me Thomas, not even Mrs Amos!" May was quite sure of her intention.

"If she does say a word to you, tell me and I will deal with her myself!" warned Thomas in jest.

"You must be careful Thomas or she may box your ears!" May laughed as she reached across and gently patted each of his ears mimicking the threats of Mrs Amos.

"Not with you to protect me, May. I hold no fear when I am with you!" said Thomas.

They kissed and hugged each other as the carriage made its way back towards Freshwater, back to May's place of employ. She felt a surging rush of passion running through her body and wished the embrace would never end.

Chapter Six

Michal had not been in good health for some time now. His mother had warned that he had been trying to cram in too much within one day. His sons George and Jacob had been annoying him of late and he had lost his temper on several occasions leaving him mentally, as well as physically, drained. As the children had grown up around her, Mrs Morey became in more desperately need of help rearing them. Their energy vastly overtook her failing health. Her neighbour at a nearby farm had offered on several occasions to have the children whilst Mrs Morey was able to have time to herself for rest. She was feeling the strain and the years were creeping up on her at an alarming rate.

❧

Mrs Morey's caring neighbour was Widow Small who lived with her son, Reuben who farmed at Steans Farm across the valley. She was a kindly soul, a true Christian who adored children, being amongst them and watching over them. Reuben was a quiet man, engulfed with many labouring duties on the land, he was always on hand to help tend the animals or assist Mary at Sullens should the need ever arise.

❧

To Mary Morey, she had always been known at the Widow Small, only a few of the more elderly members of the parish remembered her husband, though many felt the need best to forget him as rumours made him out to be a sinister character. The widow never spoke of her late husband or of his demise, so many folk felt it best never to raise the matter. One morning Mrs Morey saw the Widow Small walking in Coach Lane back to Steans after a visit to Arreton for provisions. She was carrying two heavily laden baskets of goods; Mary stopped and offered to help her carry them.

"Good morning to you Widow Small; tis a beautiful day!" called out Mrs Morey. "Do you need a hand with those panniers? Looks like you've stocked up for the winter there!"

"Morning to you to Mary, yes tis beautiful, spring is nigh. God has made sure of that. Be aware though, these panniers won't get the better of *me*!" She declared, readjusting her grip ensuring she would manage.

"And how are your family? How are you yourself Mary?" She noticed how anxious Mrs Morey looked.

"Could be better if I'm at all honest, I really need some help Widow. The boys are lovely but I am not getting any younger and it seems to me that they need more and more care than I can give them," Mary sighed witheringly. She looked ashamed and stared bleakly at the ground. There was a brief silence between the two women.

"Don't you fret Mary, bring them round to me tomorrow, I will look after them for you. The farm is sometimes a quiet place when my boy is out all day working over yonder, I'd love the company and it will make me feel that I can help you in some way," announced Widow Small.

"You're too kind Widow Small, but it would help me ten-fold, more than you know and the children will enjoy playing on your farm," said Mary with a noticeable tone of relief in her voice. She smiled gratefully at Widow Small who, in turn nodded her acceptance of her forthcoming task.

"Tomorrow morning tis then, send them round, sooner the better, they can be of use to me, feeding the calves, tending the pigs, might even find them some food, if they behave!" said the Widow as she bustled passed Mrs Morey, her panniers groaning with the weight of contents, the wicker aching with each footstep she made towards Steans.

"Must get on now, I have some baking to do!" She laughed.

Mrs Morey smiled after the old lady as she waddled down the lane, her long skirts dragging on one side as she finished her journey. Mary watched her as she turned off the lane toward Steans and thought to herself what a fine example she portrayed of sheer kindness. Never one to be selfish, the widow *always* put others before herself.

༅

Mrs Morey walked back up the path to Sullens, and stopped at the door and stared around her. This was her home, her solitude. She had seen some lovely times and some sad times at this house. Her family growing up and move away, family returning back to their roots. She thought of Michal and the loss of Beth and her pain of losing Henry, in his absence she was the backbone of strength to the whole family. How much everyone relied upon her to keep sanity firmly in its place. How hard she tried. She sighed and opened the front door, stepping inside she walked into the kitchen and placed her basket on well-scrubbed oak table.

There was an air of peacefulness about the place, the children were outside playing, and Michal was working at the wood as always. So she decided to spend her time resting until the children's return. She thought of Widow Small's kindness and she looked forward to the prospect of help from the old lady giving her a little more time to herself. She sat down and dozed off into a hapless slumber. Not long after she felt a draft of cold air fill the room and the sounds of footsteps in the parlour. A voice she instantly recognised called out, "Nanna! Nanna! Where are you?"

Mrs Morey slowly opened her eyes and focused on a young woman, she smiled and gradually coming round from her nap saw her beloved little May!

"Oh Nanna, how are you? Tis lovely to see you, I have missed you so, it has been so long!"

Little May sang out the words as she was so pleased to see her. She almost danced in delight at seeing the old lady.

"Little May! My lord, how you have grown, you are truly beautiful!" sighed Mrs Morey in delight as she rose to her feet and tightly hugged her grand daughter. Her granddaughter that had left at such a young, tender age and who now stood before her as a young woman.

"You should have let me know somehow, to expect you and pray, who is this fine gentleman?" Mrs Morey asked as she saw Thomas step quietly into the room, he didn't want to ruin Mary's reunion or shock her by his appearance.

"This, Nanna, is my... husband, Thomas Dove. We were married at Freshwater two months ago. Thomas, this is my grandmother, Mary Morey," said May, her pride burst out from her tiny frame.

"A true pleasure it is to meet you Mrs Morey. To meet the person to whom May has not stopped talking about!" said Thomas delicately kissing Mrs Morey's outstretched hand.

"Good day to you, Thomas. I am overcome by all this news. Are you staying for a while? We have a lot of catching up to do! A lot of talking. Well it must be three years since you left Sullens May. How the time flies! Let me prepare some food and we can get to know one another Thomas. I cannot take all this in," said Mrs Morey, her delight was all too apparent and she bustled in different directions not knowing really what to do first.

"Where is father?" asked May.

Mrs Morey smiled, "Where he always is, my dear, at the wood, but if not, he may be at the cottage. Why don't you go find him and bring him back to meet Thomas?" she suggested indicating to May by shaking her head to one side.

"Yes, I'll go now," said Mary and she disappeared back through the front door, slamming it shut in her haste to leave.

"She is a beautiful girl, Mrs Morey," said Thomas, "I am so lucky to have found her."

"Yes she is," said Mrs Morey, "it is wonderful to see her so happy and settled. So, tell me about yourself. What line of business are you in Thomas?"

"I run a small merchant business in Freshwater Ma'am, it is adequate for both May and my means, by that I mean that May never goes without. I make sure of that all right."

"She is lucky to have you Thomas, very lucky. You see, her background and upbringing was very hard and after her mother died; such a tragedy to lose one so young.

Beth would have adored you Thomas. She was just like May, beautiful, and full of life and not a bad bone in her!"

"May speaks often of her mother and of you, but it seems to me that the person she has missed the most has been her father. He must be a great man!" said Thomas gently probing Mrs Morey for answers to his own questions.

"You are about to find out Thomas," said Mrs Morey as she saw May and Michal approaching the front door. May led her father into the parlour, "Father, this is Thomas, my husband."

"I am pleased to meet you, sir," said Thomas offering to shake Michal's hand. Michal stood staring silently at him. The odour of tree sap filled the room. Michal moved forward and solemnly shook Thomas hand.

"Good day to you, Mister Thomas Dove." He said quietly. His eyes were not moving at all. He was transfixed. He continued to grip Thomas' hand as it seemed her was slowly taking in the fact that his daughter was now a married woman. This was the man that had taken his daughter's hand, taken her from him. He stared without blinking; a look of disbelief over came him. Thomas slowly edged away from Michal and managed to loosen his hand.

The two men stood in silence and an uneasy feeling struck Mrs Morey.

"Come on May, help me in the kitchen. They have things to discuss, leave them for a while," she warned, ushering May away, holding her by the shoulders, she gently pushed her towards the door.

Michal sat down at the hearthside and beckoned Thomas to join him. He began to rub his knee where an old injury had started to ache.

"So, where do you come from Mister Dove?" Michal enquired, his eyes still not blinking.

Thomas looked at the large, ageing woodcutter, whose shirt was spattered in blood and earth stains, his hands chapped with calluses. He swallowed carefully and replied,

"I was born at Borthwood, my parents still live there. When I was of age, I left and found work at Freshwater. Since then I run a merchant business."

"Well healed I see," answered Michal his eyes fixed once again on Thomas. He took some tobacco from his leather pouch, filling his clay pipe; lit it thoughtfully, from a twig protruding from the fire and puffed in silence filling the room with a plume of grey smoke.

"I manage, if you're worried, I am able to provide for your daughter. She has nothing to concern herself about. I mean, I keep her well," said Thomas defensively, noticing the woodcutter's disapproval of his situation. Mary had talked of her father, forewarning Thomas of his moods, his feelings and dislikes.

"As you may see, or may not see," said Michal between puffs, "I have spent my whole life outdoors, working in the copse, come wind or rain, for a few shillings a week.

We managed too yet, somehow, but life has not been kind to the likes of *me*."

"Life may not have been easy for you Mr Morey, but you have had the joy of having such a beautiful daughter, May, for that you should feel very proud and fortunate."

"Perhaps you be right there, young man. She's a good 'un, she'll treat you well, mark my words. Don't ever forget and she is as genuine as Beth was, her mother, just remember that!" Michal sat back in the chair and his mind drifted off as he thought of his wife.

Thomas smiled at the large man; he felt the woodcutter was beginning to warm to his presence. May had forewarned him of Michal's ways so he had been well prepared for their first meeting.

"Are you staying at Sullens?" asked Michal after a while sitting puffing the pipe. He took his eyes away from Thomas and gazed at the glowing embers of the fire.

"For a few days that is, if you do not mind," said Thomas. He diplomatically waited for a response; still feeling uncomfortable within the woodcutter's foreboding presence.

"Well, better make yourselves comfortable. Mother will see you are fed, the others will be back soon, they'll wanna to see you no doubt about that, the nosy beggars," remarked Michal as he thought of his children. "George aint a bad boy though…" he thought aloud.

Thomas nodded his acknowledgement and stared into the fire.

Mary and her grandmother returned to the parlour with lunch and they began to lay it upon the table.

"Must get on now," announced Michal tapping the remains of his pipe into the hearth. He rose to his feet, "I'll take nammit with me, mother."

"Can you not stay a while longer?" pleaded Mrs Morey.

"Not with the Squire's men on the look out all the time, I'm forever being watched. No, I'll be back at dusk," said Michal with finality in his voice that no one should argue with.

He walked from the room, stiffened by the period of time spent sat near the hearth, his body unused to lunch time comforts of a chair. The rest of the family heard the front door slowly close behind him.

"He works too hard for his years. I keep trying to tell him to slow down but he just won't listen to me," said Mrs Morey. She looked concerned for her son. "He works so long only to forget about Beth, it takes his mind off her. I never realised how much he actually cared for her, when she was alive he treated her badly sometimes and he never appeared to show much love for her. Since her death, he has come to realise that and now he thinks of no one else," she indicated to her guests to eat the lunch.

"How do you think he will take to Thomas?" asked May as they ate, "Do you think he'll ever warm to him?"

"May, your father would have told you by now if he didn't like Thomas. There is no need to worry your pretty self over that!" said Mrs Morey. She passed another hunk of bread to Thomas, "Here eat your fill my lad,"

❧

May smiled at her grandmother. Yet deep down she wondered if her father was just making excuses when he left, just to get out of the house to escape having to make passing conversation. She knew he thrived on solitude. She felt saddened and a little angry that he could not even make the effort as it had been the first time Thomas and he had met. She looked at her grandmother sitting as politely as she could across from Thomas at the table. It made her giggle deep inside as she saw Mrs Morey trying to eat her food with gentility and with fervour. She caught her grandmother's eye.

"Nanna, I want you to be the first to know. I am with child; it will be born in the early part of next year!" She announced. Thomas stopped eating in surprise of May's unexpected announcement. They had planned to tell both Michal and her grandmother when they were both together. Mary Morey could hardly contain her joy.

"Oh May! That is wonderful news, but should you not have told your father first?" cried Mrs Morey getting up and hugging May tightly causing her to gasp.

"To be honest Nanna, I don't think he would care," May bit her lip awaiting the response.

"How could you think that May? He will care, he will be overjoyed!" said Mrs Morey indignantly. "He loves you more than you think. He may not be the happiest of men in this world but I am sure he will be happy when you tell him, especially as this will be his first grandchild! May, go after him, tell him now, we will wait here, he will be overjoyed, please tell him, I know he will be happy!"

Her grandmother's encouragement was enough to spur Mary to leave the table and dash after her father.

"Do you want me to come with you?" called Thomas.

"No tis all right, I'll go alone," called May from the hall.

Outside, she could smell the burning of timber further up into the lane. The fumes led her to Michal working at the clearing and she made her way carefully through the trees.

"Father, can I talk to you for a while?" she asked when she finally caught up with him. He was working with his back to her.

Michal turned round and saw his daughter standing in a haze of wood smoke, for a moment he thought she looked just like Beth. He smiled when he realised and spoke softly. "Come here girl, let me hold you."

"Oh father, I have missed you so much," May cried, grabbing hold of Michal and burying her head against his chest.

"You are doing well though girl, aren't you? A fine husband with a good business, wealth, all you could wish for."

"Yes, I am very fortunate father. I have one other piece of news I want to tell you… I am with child!"

She waited for his response, her breath baited.

Michal stepped back and stared at Mary, he paused, with eyes glazed as though he had been hit. At length he spoke, his voice wavered.

"My little May, my girl with child, oh May!" He thought of the day Beth had found out she was pregnant. He pulled her close to his body. "You make me feel very happy, happy for the first time in an age, well done girl. Come on, let's get back to Sullens and tell your grandmother, she too will be happy. I'll finish this work tomorrow whatever the Squire says. To hell he may go!"

"I have already told her," said Mary hesitantly, she immediately wished she hadn't opened her mouth.

Michal looked deflated as though he had been punched from a great height, he paused and whispered.

"May, do not ever be afraid to tell me anything, anything at all do you hear? I may be miserable but don't ever feel you can't speak to me."

"I am sorry father, come on let's get back now," Mary held her father's arm as together they left the wood. Michal carried his axe by his side and they headed back to Sullens. Mrs Morey was standing in the doorway to meet them. At first she looked concerned but then her face broke into a smile as she saw the two arm in arm, with Michal visibly elated, chatting happily to May as they neared the house. Thomas stood a little way behind Mrs Morey in the hallway, he too felt anxious holding his hands clenched tightly behind his back.

"It's going to be a good year boy!" remarked Michal as he strode up to Thomas. "Especially as there is to be a young un due later on. Well done to you both, as I said to May and I'll say to you, you have made me a happy man!"

Thomas felt a sense of huge relief, glancing at Mary he stepped forward and shook Michal's rough hand.

"Thank you Mr Morey, I will make sure Mary has the best care."

"Yes, make sure of that young man, she is so precious to me, she'll need proper care," said Michal.

"I think a celebration is needed," declared Mrs Morey in delight. "We have some mead. I'll open the new cask."

"Good idea, mother," said Michal. "Come on you two," he gestured at Thomas and May, "let us rest a while and enjoy a few jars. We have some talking to do."

Mary followed her grandmother to the kitchen, "'Tis the happiest I have ever seen him, the news has truly lifted his spirit. You have gladdened a depressed man May," said Mrs Morey as she broke open the new cask of mead, the smell of alcohol permeated the kitchen and drifted towards the parlour. The two men stood in front of the hearth.

"Any thoughts of moving from Freshwater boy?" asked Michal as he picked up his still warm pipe and relit it, clenching it between his teeth.

"We have thoughts of moving, yes, but we have not decided to where or when, as May is pregnant we may wait now until after the birth."

"Well there is plenty of room here boy. Sullens has a lot of unused space, that is, if you want to live with a woodcutter, a host of children and his mother!"

"Thank you for the invitation, I will speak to May see how she feels about it. I would easily find a new place for my business in Newport," Thomas hesitated as he thought of possible implications that may arise, "Yes, I will speak to her." He added although his mind ticked over in uncertainty.

"Don't leave it too long boy, I may change my mind!" warned Michal.

"Here we are," said May as she and her grandmother carried the fresh smelling pungent mead into the parlour. A china jug brimmed full of the intoxicating liquid. She placed it on the table pouring out four glasses and gladly handed one to each person. She raised her glass, "To the unborn babe and her mother!"

"Or his!" remarked Michal as he slugged his mead in a few rapid gulps.

Mary looked across at Thomas and smiled behind her glass. Michal was truly happy!

CHAPTER SEVEN

The back garden of Sullens was a very tranquil place. At the bottom it was surrounded by an orchard and it was the home to trees of apple, pear and damson. May slowly walked through it admiring the beauty of the countryside. She took in the various pungent aromas, mainly of freshly felled trees, evergreen and oak where her father was labouring in the valley. A few brave rosebuds had survived the winter onslaught, albeit they were crisp and deadened by the frost but pale slithers of pink could just be seen adding an insipid splash of colour to the garden. It was so peaceful, looking towards the Downs, May took in a deep breathe and closing her eyes, drank in the freshness of the air as a gentle, but chilling breeze rippled through her loosely fastened hair. She pulled her shawl closely around her shoulders.

It was nearing the end of hers and Thomas rather prolonged stay at Sullens. May had enjoyed every minute with immense enthusiasm, even though she had felt tired most of the time from her state of health. She adored being amongst her family once more. It had been such a long time since she had first left for Freshwater. She smiled secretly to herself as she heard her grandmother in the scullery singing an indistinguishable, yet beautiful song. She lingered for a while by a window that was slightly ajar for it was such a lovely, mellow song, one she remembered from her childhood that her grandmother always recited and Mary knew that she was feeling happy. A startled blackbird flew out from one of the leafless trees in the orchard, cheeping in a birdlike protest. Mary gasped as she felt hands on her shoulders. She hadn't heard Thomas creeping up behind her. She turned around; opening her eyes she began to giggle.

"Hello my beauty, what are you doing out here? You'll catch a chill."

"I was just listening to Grandmother singing. It sounds so lovely," sighed May and once again she closed her eyes, turning her back to Thomas, she rested the back of her head on his chest as he placed his hands back upon her shoulders, gently kissing her neck.

"It is a lovely song," He paused to listen, "Sullens; I know is a peaceful place. It seems to be a happy home; even your father seems content of late."

Thomas released his hold of May and walked on in front of her. He stopped suddenly and turned to face her.

"May…" he paused taking a deep breathe, "when we first arrived here, I did not warm to your father, or should I say, he did not exactly accept or care to know me. I suppose I cannot blame his feeling after all, his daughter leaving as a child, returning as a married woman to a man he had not even met. It must have shocked him. After a time, he did talk of us and where we would live." He stopped to take in Mary's reaction. He had just intimated that her father had been the guilty party in their strained relationship.

May appeared surprised.

"Father and you talked of moving? What are you talking of?" she remained still, her eyes wide and completely focussed on Thomas, "Tell me Thomas, don't hide anything from me!"

"As if I ever could my dearest," he smiled wryly at his young wife who stood before him defiantly, hands on hips, her shawl slipped to expose her neck. Thomas looked briefly about him as he continued.

"I told him my thoughts of moving and, now you are with child, maybe it would make more sense to move before the birth. Your father asked if we would care to move in with him and your grandmother here at Sullens. I told him I would confirm with him after discussing it with you."

May's eyes lit up as she exclaimed, "Thomas are you sure? Would you not mind? What of your business?"

"Questions, always so many questions," laughed Thomas as May spun round in a circle, like a small child, she danced with joy. Suddenly she stopped and asked outright.

"Thomas, would you truly be happy here? It would mean *so* much to Nanna and to father, I think it would much more to father. Nanna I know would be so happy; she could help me at the birth of the babe. How would you feel? I know you don't agree with all father says, his ways and all...."

Thomas placed his finger on her lips, "If it makes you happy, May," he leant forward and kissed her forehead, "Then I too am happy!"

"Oh, Thomas!"

She flung her arms around his neck, burying her head into his shoulder. Thomas was relieved of May's happiness, as always she was foremost in his actions. He put his own doubts far to the back of his mind.

"When your father returns tonight, I will speak with him and arrange everything," said Thomas, "you just concentrate on looking after that child of mine and get your rest!"

"I love you so much, Thomas," said May, holding both his hands in her tiny palms, "Come, let's go indoors its getting cold now."

Thomas led her back through the garden as the squawking blackbird flew high over their heads to rest in a nearby laurel bush to continue his earth shattering performance.

It was a few weeks into the New Year and winter had slowly begun to shake off its cold, icy grip and early signs of spring had started to appear around Sullens. May had spent the past few days confined to her bed for rest upon the Doctor's order. She had been feeling the cold and Thomas reminded her that she had probably caught a chill spending time in the garden. Although the day had been dry and clear, it was still only mid-February and cold, even for a stroll in the garden. Her grandmother helped to keep May comfortable and as warm as possible as she did have a slight fever. May was presented with piping hot bowls of soup to keep her warm and to boost her flagging energy, but still she showed signs of exhaustion.

Thomas was relieved that May was being well cared for by her grandmother. It enabled him to continue working at his business as much as possible but the strain of the weekly journey to from Freshwater to Newport made him think seriously about moving the business into Newport as soon as he could, close to their new home. He wanted to spend as much time with May as he could.

Thomas and May had been living at Sullens since earlier in the winter. Michal had not made comment on their presence but on a few occasions, Thomas was a little uneasy and sensed inwardly that Michal was annoyed at his space being constantly crowded. It was if the first invitation of moving in had been given half-heartedly and now the idea didn't seem so amiable after all. One evening, as they shared one another's company in the parlour, Michal looked up and commented idly on how Thomas' business was fairing.

"Quite well thank you, Michal for asking. It has been busy since Christmas time, I have received some promising news on new orders for the springtime," replied Thomas, as he felt enthused that Michal was possibly showing an interest in his affairs.

"Oh! Seems you just have to click you fingers and money just comes to ya!" scoffed Michal. He had had another bad day and was feeling the need to vent his frustration on someone and that happened to be Thomas.

His remark greatly annoyed Thomas and he moved restlessly in his chair.

"It is not a case of *sitting* and *waiting* for it to fall at my feet, Michal. There is lots of negotiating to do on my behalf....." Michal interrupted Thomas.

"I don't want to be bored with all that fancy talk, with a language I can't understand boy!" he sneered, wiping his nose with an air of ignorance. He childishly felt that he couldn't even look Thomas in the face as he faced up for an exchange of heated words. Instead he looked into the hearth and the glowing chunks of wood that burnt slowly without any effort.

Thomas cleared his throat. Feeling undaunted by this verbal onslaught, he uncrossed his legs and faced Michal.

"In layman's terms, so you might *just* understand what I'm saying, I mean I have much talking to do with my customers. It takes tact and confidence; that is why it works."

"Never worked for me, all that jabber," Michal looked away sulkily. He felt belittled by Thomas' expertise with words he never even knew or used.

"With respect Michal, you probably have never had the chance," said Thomas in what he hoped had sounded like a kind observation to Michal and not an insult. He sat back into his chair and waited for the response.

Michal's eyes instantly flashed with anger.

"How *dare* you put me down! You're soundin' like Squire Cheke, looking at me like I'm an idiot. I may not be able to read nor write nor talk proper to people, but I've never stopped trying to earn my living as honest as I can. How dare you talk to me like that in my own house as well, my house, not your house, MINE!!" Michal got up in a frenzy. He shook with rage.

"I am sorry Michal, you don't understand. I wasn't trying to hurt your feelings," reasoned Thomas, he looked a little shocked at Michal's unexpected outburst and stepped back from the woodcutter.

"Just watch you tongue Thomas Dove, I may not be as young as I used to be, but I still know how to weald my axe!" Michal stormed out of the room, almost knocking his mother sideways as he met her in the hallway.

"Out of my way, Mother!" he bellowed brushing her aside in his anger. He strode angrily to the front door.

"Michal! What on earth is the matter?" asked Mary Morey in surprise.

"Ask *Dove*, he'll tell you, I can't tell you, I'm not clever enough with my words and talk!" he roared, slamming the door behind him, making the whole house shudder with the force of his anger.

Thomas rushed into the hallway.

"I am afraid Michal misunderstood what I was saying. I am fully to blame, Mrs Morey."

"Don't worry, Thomas," she sighed in dismay. "Michal can be very stubborn and he has not been in the best of moods lately. He'll be fine later. I am going up to see May for a while," she reassured Thomas and led him slowly back to the parlour.

ↄ

Mary smiled weakly and left him alone. Thomas sat back into his chair and gazed into the hearth. He watched the orange and red flames begin crackle in the grate, as though they too were having their own argument. He could feel the heat quite hot against his face, was it just the fire or had his own anger made him suddenly perspire? He picked up another log and pushed it deep into the glowing embers, hard into the flames. Suddenly he heard his name being called. It was May's voice from upstairs. He quickly ran upstairs to her room and nearly fell over Mrs Morey who was lying in the doorway.

May was crying.

"Oh Thomas, send for the doctor, quickly, she just collapsed, she seems to be hardly breathing!"

Thomas stared in horror; he turned and ran back downstairs, his heart beating at fever pitch. As he rushed out into the lane he saw Michal striding off into the distance. He shrieked at the top of his voice, "Michal! Michal!"

Michal ignored the shouts and continued to walk his pace quickened.

"Michal! For god's sake man, it's your mother, she has collapsed! We need to get the Doctor quickly!" yelled Thomas, hoping he could stop Michal in time before he disappeared.

Michal stopped in his tracks, he swung round, "Mother? Collapsed?"

"Yes," Thomas caught up with him completely breathless. His chest hurt as he talked. "Get the doctor and I'll get back to the house!" He panted.

"No! I'll go back to the house. You go fetch the doctor. He lives in the village next to the church. I'm going to get back to my mother," said Michal as the anger had suddenly changed to fear, which built up in his pulsating heart.

He had always dreaded the day that anything happened to his mother, although he knew deep down, it would come to haunt him. Michal realised his nightmare was becoming fact.

"As you wish, Michal. Hurry please, it does not look good and May is beside herself with worry! It's not good, not for her health and the baby."

As Michal reached Sullens he could hear May screaming from upstairs.

"Oh please, somebody please help, help quickly!" Her voice was pitiful and distressed.

"It's all right, girl!" called Michal. "I am here!"

When he reached the top of the stairs he found his mother on the floor laying crumpled and still.

"Oh father, she just fell without any warning. Here put this blanket round her to keep her warm. I am helpless I cannot get out of this wretched bed," wept May and she weakly threw a blanket from her bed.

"Lie still!" ordered Michal, "you are in no fit state girl."

"Father, what is wrong with her, where is Thomas? I must help, I must!" May edged herself to the side of the bed and promptly fell awkwardly to the floor.

"For God's sake girl, why did you move? I can't see to both of ye. Here, grab my hand."

Michal left his mother's side and clasped his arms around his delirious daughter and placed her back on the bed, covering her with an edge of blanket.

"Where is *that* Thomas Dove?"

May groaned in agony, pains in her stomach had begun and she clutched her body tightly, shivering with cold.

From what seemed like an age afterwards there was a noise downstairs of the door slamming. It was Thomas with the Doctor; they both ran quickly up to the bedroom.

"Hello, Michal. Oh lord, right, Thomas please help me move her into the hallway."

Thomas and Michal stood silently watching whilst the Doctor attended Mrs Morey. He stood up and faced them looking grave. He removed his spectacles and rubbed his eyes.

"Michal, I am so sorry, but she is dead. She seems to have suffered heart failure; there is nothing anyone could have done. I am so sorry; I will make the necessary arrangements when I get back to Arreton. Thomas can you stay with young May? The poor girl is in shock, this will not help the baby at all. I will attend her now. Michal what has happened to her?"

Michal stood in disbelief.

"But she was all right earlier on; she showed no signs of illness!" He blurted out thinking back to his outburst as he'd pushed his mother out of the way. His thoughts relived Beth's last day and how she had continued on regardless of her failing health.

"Michal, heart failure never does show, it just happens and quickly. If it is any comfort to you, she would have felt no pain at all. It was very sudden and over with immediately, always remember that. What about May?" asked the doctor, he looked concerned and needed to know what had happened to her.

"Um… she fell, out of the bed, trying to help her grandmother. I… um, just put her back in the bed again…"

Michal was distant; shocked at his mother's body lying at his feet. The person he loved and doted on. The person that had always been there, in times of trouble and need. No longer, now only a body; a shell. The spirit flushed from it. No more life with that one person, the anchor of the whole family. He turned away. He breathed shallowly and bent his head in sorrow, silently weeping.

Thomas knelt at May's bedside, holding her hand, watching as the doctor checked her breathing and examining for any bruising. He looked slightly less worried.

"I think it's the shock, she will be all right; just give her time. Don't leave her Thomas, stay with her. Perhaps send for the Widow Small, she will attend to May."

The doctor collected his overcoat and hat. He patted Michal sympathetically on the shoulder and asked, "Michal… are you all right?"

Michal nodded. He held tightly onto the banister, his face was pale and he was distant. He muttered to himself, "There is a curse on this house… there must be a curse on me." He began to walk down the stairs. He turned to the doctor.

"Doctor, thank you for your trouble, did you say you will make the arrangements?"

"Yes, Michal, that is the least I can do. Mary was a good friend to me over the years. I too feel the terrible sadness of her passing like this. Thomas will help you as well. It may be an idea for you to ask Widow Small to come over now and help care for you, May and the children until things can get back to normal."

"I'll go there now and ask," volunteered Michal and he stumbled out through the front door, leaving Sullens in a sense of total despair. He soon reached Steans Farm and found the Widow Small in her front yard feeding the fowls, throwing grain from her apron, casting pearls of barley across the yard as the birds stampeded in every direction trying to greedily peck up every morsel of food.

"Hello Michal Morey! What on *earth* brings you to Steans?" called Widow Small in surprise as Michal hardly ever visited her. She stopped throwing the grain.

"Bad news I am afraid, Widow. Its mother… she is… dead." Michal's voice slowly croaked the words out half in disbelief, half in sorrow.

"Oh good lord above! You poor man! Poor, dear Mary, God rest her soul."

Widow Small quickly emptied her apron of remaining grain and pushed the fowls aside, making them cluck angrily at being interrupted from their feed.

"I need help with young May, she is poorly with this child, she saw it all, terrible shock to her. Can you come and sit with her awhile, try and calm her?" asked Michal, tears began to prick his eyes once more as he talked.

"Of course, I'll come back with you now. Poor Mary, God rest her soul and young May, what a shock!" She patted down her apron making sure all the grain had dispersed and yelled back towards the farmhouse, "I'll be at Sullens for the time being Reuben, there has been a tragedy!"

Reuben ran to the front of the house.

"What has happened Mother?" He called out.

"Michal's mother has passed on; I'm going to help at Sullens."

"I am sorry to hear that Michal, God be with you," replied Reuben gravely; he removed his hat in respect. He looked at Michal who stared at the ground. The reality was beginning to sink in.

"Come on Michal, lets away now," urged the Widow Small pushing Michal forward.

"I'm going back to the cottage for a while, need some time alone," announced Michal.

"Are you sure? Don't you think May needs you? Don't you think she would like some comforting? What of the children?" Widow Small was concerned about Michal and his request to be alone when there were others to think about as well as himself.

"That's *your* job Widow!" yelled Michal instantly turning on the old woman, "Just leave me be!"

"As you wish, Michal. I'll not argue against ya." The widow continued to walk towards Sullens. She was quite used to Michal's outbursts and his moods having spent many years as his neighbour.

At Sullens, Thomas was talking with the doctor.

"Make sure May is not left alone tonight, I've made her comfortable but she is in severe shock. It could start the baby off early, if it does, send for me straight away," warned the doctor.

"Yes, I will Doctor and thank you," said Thomas. He shook the doctor's hand in gratitude.

"I will ask John Hance of Arreton, the undertaker, to call later this afternoon to take Mary's body away and then we must arrange for the funeral. Where is Michal?"

The front door opened, "Hello, tis Widow Small from Steans here!" The Widow called out ruefully.

"Ah, Widow Small, we are in the parlour, please come in!" called Thomas.

"Sorry to meet you in such a sad circumstance, Doctor, where is the girl?"

"Upstairs, she is asleep at the moment," replied the doctor. "Is Michal with you?"

"He's gone to the cottage," said Widow Small, "best leave him be, now I'll go sit with young May, I'll sit with her as long as needed." Widow Small slowly made her way upstairs.

∽

Noticing the door opened to Mrs Morey's bedroom, she quietly looked inside to see the body lying on the bed, arms folded, shrouded by a white blanket. She drew near and knelt by the side of the bed and whispered a prayer. She slowly got up and struck her chest in the sign of the cross. She moved to the window and released the catch letting cold air into the room.

"We had some good times old girl. I'll never forget thee." The Widow gently touched Mrs Morey's still warm hand. "May you rest in peace…"

She slowly left the room, closing the door behind her. She walked into the neighbouring bedroom and sat near May's bed gazing at her.

"Poor child, poor dear girl," she gently smoothed May's forehead and continued to talk in reassuring hushed whispers.

"I must be away now, do not forget that John Hance will be here as soon as possible," the doctor reminded Thomas.

"Thank you once again doctor," said Thomas.

"Goodbye and my sincere condolences to you all." The doctor left Sullens in silence.

He felt very sorry to see his old friend die in such a sudden way. He would truly miss her, a kinder woman you could not have wished to meet. He travelled back along Coach Lane and, as he passed Michal's cottage, he hesitated but then decided it was best to leave Michal alone and not to harass him in his hour of despair, it would only make him worse.

လ

Only a few weeks had passed by since Mary Morey's funeral and May Dove had begun to feel pains in her stomach. She was trying to wash some clothes in the back scullery when she suddenly grabbed her stomach as sharp pains began to overcome her and sap every drop of energy. She carefully knelt on to the floor; her breath seemed to be escaping from her body as she tried to stay calm.

She swallowed slowly.

"This must be my time now," she whispered, half in hope that someone may hear her. She closed her eyes tightly shut, biting her lower lip in agony. Perhaps the pains would go away.

"Please dear God, help me. I need you, please don't forsake me now," she opened her eyes momentarily to see her brother George stood in the doorway.

"You be alright, Little May?" he asked looking a little alarmed to see his sister on the floor.

May summoned the courage to speak.

"Get father, Georgy, get him now, I beg of you!" She panted, just as another unforgiving pain shot through her body, "Arrgh! Dear Lord, help me!"

"He aint about sis, he gawn to the Inn," George's young face paled in an instance.

"You be bleeding May! I got to get help now!" His eyes were wide as a patch of red appeared around the back of May's skirts.

"Just get anyone! Find the Widow Small, anyone I don't care who!" she yelled in exasperation.

George dashed from the scullery as May slowly got to her feet. By this time her skirts were drenched in blood making her feel so uncomfortable and weakening with every breath. She crept forward with both hands clasped to her stomach, her body completely bent double like an old woman with crumbling bones, falling from one side to another into the walls. Each step an agonising burden as the pains began once more. She reached the parlour and collapsed to the floor just as George returned with Widow Small following closely behind.

"May! Dear lord," the widow found May in a heap on the floor, "George, go to the doctor, there's a good boy, be quick as you can now, take the mare, she be in the back paddock. Tell the doctor May's babe is coming, be quick now!"

"Yes, Widow Small, soon as I can, I'll be back!" George's concerned pale face caught sight of May lying on the floor and he scuttled back out, slamming the door firmly shut behind him. He stood briefly at the gateway, his little heart beating rapidly in his chest. He tried to compose himself as he remembered the blood on the floor and the distress that May was in. A vision that he would, in later years, always remember.

Widow Small knelt beside May.

"Its all right May, I'm here; I'll help you now. I'll just get some blankets and water, make you comfortable."

Widow Small anxiously searched for bedding and filled a pail of water from the well. Fortunately May had lit the fire earlier in the kitchen and it was well established so she quickly put a pot of water onto to boil, slopping it onto the embers making the fire hiss its protest at being disturbed. She returned to the parlour. May hadn't moved an inch. She remained clutching her stomach.

Fresh evidence of blood had oozed onto the floorboards staining the wood.

"Here put this round your shoulders and I'll bolster this blanket under your head. How are you feeling May? May can you hear me girl?"

The widow gently shook Mary who was drifting in and out of consciousness.

"Widow, I'm in pain, so much pain, I can't hardly breath there's so much pain. I wish Nanna was here, she would know what to do, and she'd help me. Please God bring her back! Please!" Mary drifted off again, her mind clearly not functioning as she began to talk to her grandmother again and again.

"You got to stay awake May. You needs to, to have this babe, you can't sleep. Doctor's on his way. He'll be here soon, don't you fret, he'll help." Widow Small shook May trying desperately to keep her awake.

May had broken out into a cold sweat, "Widow, I'm so cold, so *very* cold," she complained.

"You be all right May, it's just the babe. You'll be better once it's born. Take's all yer strength and you got to be strong May, so strong." Widow Small tried to calm her. She stroked May's hand and periodically wiped the sweat from her forehead. Her hair was drenched in perspiration.

"Where's Thomas?" May gasped amidst the contractions, "Is he here?"

"When the Doctor gets here, I'll get my boy to go search for him. Is he far do you know?"

"He had to be in Newport today, far as I know. Send for him Widow. I need him here now," May reached out to the widow's hand and weakly squeezed it.

Widow Small held her small hand and reassured her.

"All right May, we'll find him, I make sure of that for you."

Within the hour, George returned with the Doctor who immediately ushered them from the room so he could be alone with May. Widow Small was kept busy carrying pails of water from the well and following the Doctor's orders when he summoned her.

Thomas was sought and quickly returned to Sullens to be with his wife. Late that same afternoon, May gave birth to a baby boy. Thomas was overjoyed. They named him James.

Soon after the birth, the Doctor took Thomas to one side and showed his concern over May's failing health. He explained that May was not the strongest of women and the pregnancy and the birth had taken its toll on her well-being. Thomas refused to believe that May's life may be in danger as he felt the Doctor was over reacting as he was still mourning the death of Mrs Morey like all the rest of the family.

But the vale of death had decided to cast its untimely shadow over May Dove. She did not recover. After losing so much blood, a month after the birth of James, she died in the arms of her beloved Thomas in the early hours. Refusing to let his wife's body go, Thomas remained with her all that night. Widow Small, who had been looking after May and her baby, stood in the doorway of the bedroom, holding the tiny bundle in her arms, rocking him gently trying to fight back her own tears. She had to show strength. She had to, for Thomas, the children and for Michal's sake.

❧

Michal remained silent throughout May's funeral service at St George's Church. His mind drifting back to the day May had been baptised there. He gazed towards the pulpit and the large stone font. She had been so tiny and she had behaved beautifully whilst the priest performed the service. No more than a few days old… Thomas was stood beside Michal, his eyes filled with tears; he looked at the floor then to the vast eaves in the roof as the service continued. James quietly gurgled in the Widow Small's arms. It was almost as though he sensed the grief about him. Thomas glanced at Michal and saw how helpless and aged he had become. The once strong, thick-set frame of the burly woodcutter was now bent and vulnerable. His hair, lank and unkempt; his face, gaunt and deeply troubled. Thomas looked toward the alter; he saw the coffin laid in front of it, his beloved May laying inside. He remembered the day that he first saw her at Freshwater and he smiled to himself as he saw the young girl plucking countless pheasants in the scullery. He suddenly heard his name called, "Mr Dove… if you please."

The priest had summoned Thomas to read the lesson. Thomas tried to focus on the pulpit and addressed the congregation as best he could. He could hear his own voice talking of May and her brief life, but it was all in a haze of garbled and incomprehensible noise. It didn't make much sense as he slowly returned to his seat alongside Michal. He could see many people in the congregation but could not focus on any of their faces.

e/s

As the coffin was lowered deep into the earth, next to her mother's grave, later in the churchyard, Thomas threw a handful of earth on top of it. There was a large group of people around the grave, many sobbing, supporting each other in this time of grief. He could see Michal staring into space, who was holding a bunch of flowers that had wilted in his grasp.

"Come Michal, lets go back home now," said Thomas gently touching Michal's arm.

"How can I *ever* call Sullens home now?" asked Michal sadly, his eyes still staring ahead of him. His voice quivered as he spoke in barely more than a whisper.

"It *is* your home Michal, you have told me before, it *is* your home." Thomas stood beside him as the people began to filter away from the graveside, having paid their last respects.

"It used to be, before all this," sighed Michal. He replaced his hat precariously on his head.

"Think of baby James, he needs us both now. He is *our* family," said Thomas putting his hand on Michal's shoulder.

"Perhaps so," replied Michal and he walked away from the grave, "I will see you back there later," he added.

"There is not such a troubled man as Michal Morey," remarked Widow Small, as she stood by Thomas' side. James lay asleep in her arms.

"No, I do not suppose there is, but my heart is truly broken Widow Small. I'll never get over her….never. Part of me… I feel… has gone with her…" Thomas walked towards the waiting carriage.

"Here I will hold the babe whilst you climb up," he reached out and took hold of the baby.

"Thank you, Thomas," said the Widow, "take us back to Sullens, Reuben." She instructed her own son, who picked up the reins and clicked his tongue to make the horse move on. Further up the lane they reached Michal who was walking slowly back.

"Need a ride Michal?" asked the Widow as they drew up along side him.

"I'll make me own way, thanking you, Widow," he replied and continued on up the hill.

They travelled on in silence back to Sullens. Michal walked on up to the Hare and Hounds at the top of the hill. On seeing him arrive, the landlord Jed plied Michal with a flagon of ale.

"You've had a tough time haven't you old man, wonder you keep sane with it all!" said Jed sympathetically.

"I wonder myself, Jed. It was bad when Beth died, but father, then mother and now my child, my Little May, I cannot seem to see a way out of this vale of death!"

"Time, they say Michal, heals," replied Jed wisely, trying to appreciate the situation.

"I wish it were me, I really do," whispered Michal. "I now have a babe with no mother to care for it, and Thomas who cares only for his work. I do not know what will become of us."

"God bless you Michal," murmured Jed as he placed his hand on the woodcutter's shoulder and walked away from him. No one could have imagined the despair that Michal felt as he sat alone in the corner of the Inn with only a mug of ale to comfort his grief.

CHAPTER EIGHT

Thomas had tried so hard to rebuild his shattered life by throwing himself deeply into his work. It had been some years now since the death of May but he couldn't seem to recover from his despair. He worked long hours so that he didn't have to go back to Sullens until late. Some nights he would fall asleep at his desk and awaken only to find that he had been there all night. Widow Small had taken over caring for James, who was now a growing boy, but she had begun to tire of late. She was the vital support that both Michal and Thomas were desperate for. However, she herself was getting on in years and was in need of rest. Michal remained ever silent. He spent much time sitting alone at his cottage where only the bravest of souls would venture out to visit him. On one of their now more increasingly frequent visits to Sullens, George, Michal's eldest son and his wife, Grace were concerned over Widow Small's involvement with James.

George felt he needed to discuss with Michal the baby's future and deal with the implications that would grow along with the child. He decided to call upon Michal at his cottage and see if the old man would see reason to his proposed request. When he arrived, the cottage door was open, a trail of rain water had gathered in the tiny hallway. George called out into the darkness.

"Father! Are you there? Its George, I need to speak with you."

"Yes boy, I am here," was the gruff but distant reply, "in the back room."

George walked through the narrow passage toward the kitchen; there was an air of damp and the smell of mustiness overcame the whole cottage. He found his father slumped at the kitchen table, a few tired embers burnt in the hearth and was the only source of light in that depressing room.

"Sit down, boy, not seen you for a while, how are you?" asked Michal without looking at George

"I fair well thank you father, what about you?" George looked at his father and felt a surge of sadness as he watched the woodcutter gradually sit upright.

"What do you think?" growled Michal.

"It is so dark and cold in here father, let me find a candle to shed some light at least." He got up and began to search about in the half-light, "Do you know where they might be?" he asked.

"Ask Beth, she knows where they are," whispered Michal as he resumed his slumped position.

"Why do you mention mother?" Asked George in surprise, "You have not talked much of her since she died."

"She is on my mind boy, her spirit keeps me company, that is why I like to spend time here…with her," said Michal.

George edged towards the scullery feeling his way in the gloom, his hair brushed against cobwebs that hung from the ceiling in large grey veils. He shivered as the thoughts of the lurking spiders and vermin but continued his search.

"What are you doing boy?" boomed Michal unexpectedly as he slammed his hands down on the table.

"For God's sake boy, sit down and stop scrabbling about! You sound like the rats creepin' about!"

"I'm just trying to find the candles father, to give some cheer to this place," reasoned George. He found a half burnt candle and lit the wick from the hearth and the kitchen was immediately plunged into a vision of light. The glimmering flame suddenly plunged the room into a cheering haze of yellow, transforming the kitchen. George smiled to himself.

"That's better now, father, can see you proper now!" George tried to amuse the old man.

"There is no cheer in this place, that's long gone, for sure boy," Michal continued to stare in front of him. His eyes were lifeless and sunken in from his cheekbones.

"The day Beth died was the day that I too died… but, I am still left here to cope with the ghosts. Can't you see 'em, leerin' at me… all the time… they haunt my soul. I can't even move without them forever in my way."

Michal stared about him looking into the darkened corners of the room, desperately searching for phantoms. The phantoms that rocked his very soul to the core. George was convinced Michal thought they watched over him. The cottage was indeed a miserable shrine to Beth, something that she wouldn't have wanted if she were alive. George knew his mother would have shuddered at the state of the place and of the condition of Michal and his mind that had slowly begun to deteriorate to such an extent that George felt questionable over his father's sanity.

"Do you see them now, father?" asked George as he placed the candle on the table illuminating Michal's drawn features. The shadows on his face highlighting the lines that lay like furrows on a ploughed field amidst his visage.

"I always see 'em; father, mother, Beth and now… May. They are always here, always talking, tormenting me…" Michal's eyes filled with tears. "You won't believe how many times they ask me. To be with em… leave this…. hell hole I'm in…."

"Go where?" asked George in confusion. He placed his hand on Michal's arm.

"To be with them, that is all they keeps on asking me. God only knows I've thoughts of going. There is nothing to stop me. What have I here? A dark stinking cottage, Sullens that I don't even own. A job that I hate; the Squire who I despise. What's the point?" Michal wiped away the tears that stained his face, with the back of his hand.

"You still have your family, father. You still have us, me and Grace, Jacob and Thomas and baby James," said George firmly.

"Don't think Thomas counts now, he's too busy with his work. Now Little May's gone, he doesn't want to be at Sullens and he has lost interest in the boy too," said Michal and he looked pitifully at his son.

George sat heavily on a chair next to Michal.

"That is why I have come to talk with you, about... James," he announced.

"What's wrong with the boy? Not sick is he?" asked Michal in horror, concern overcame his face.

"No, the boy is fine. It's the Widow Small. She's not fairing so well, the boy is making her tired, she needs rest now. Don't forget that she is old, father," George tried to make Michal understand the problem.

"Yes, I suppose I've left it all to her to deal with. I can't bring myself to be in that house, too many ghosts, like this place, just too many!" He gestured round the room to the imaginary phantoms.

"I have thought whether you would like Grace and me to look after James. We could stay at Sullens for a time, I can help you with your work, Squire won't know, what do you think?" asked George, he dare hardly breathe as he waited for Michal to respond.

Michal looked up at George; he wiped his face on his dirty, torn sleeve. He spoke after a lengthy silence.

"It would be the answer, I suppose," he smiled weakly at George, he appreciated the gesture.

"Then that is settled," declared George. He got up from the table.

"I'll go now and take the news to Thomas and the Widow and arrange everything."

"As you wish, my boy." Michal was nonplussed.

"Father, try to think of the boy's welfare, not just yourself. It will help with your own grief," George tried to reason with Michal and to give encouragement for him to have something to live for.

"I'll try, boy. Better get that nipper to the church and have him baptised. Aint been baptised. Should've been baptised. Tell Grace to contact the Parson, arrange for it," added Michal who had begun to show a little more interest in the situation.

George smiled at his father. He hoped he could regenerate that fighting 'Morey spirit' in his old bones. Michal slowly got up out of his chair, scraping it across the floor.

"May even have time for an ale or two at the Inn!" he added rubbing his shoulder. He walked across to the pantry, "Fancy some cheese, boy?"

"No, I'll be away to Sullens thank you, father," George said as he walked towards the door. He closed it slowly behind him and he felt at least he had achieved something with Michal. He sighed and thought of the weathered and beaten frame of his father, a man wreaked in grief, stooped into the depths of misery, precariously perched on the edge of his sanity. He would try all he could to cheer Michal up. He walked towards Sullens and he thought of the Widow Small and how glad she would be to have someone to take over bringing up for James.

"That is wonderful news, George!" exclaimed the Widow as George gave her the news. "How did you convince your father?"

"It did not take much, once father realised what was happening. He is living in a world of his own at that place. He sees ghosts of all the family. He was telling me that they keep on wanting him to go with them. He is in a sorry state, Widow Small..." George broke off. He felt he should not reveal too much of Michal's plight to his neighbour, it may only reach the gossips of the village and create more misery for Michal.

"And Thomas, is he agreeable to the arrangement?" asked Widow Small in curiosity.

"I'll be speaking with him tonight, but rest assured Widow Small, it won't be a problem," George smiled down at the elderly widow.

He added, "Grace will enjoy motherhood!"

"It's not that I don't love the child, far from it. He is an angel and growing so very fast. It does not seem long since his birth, but he is spirited and has much strength.

Anyway I'll be off, don't forget, I'm only at *Steans*, if you need me at all, just remember that," urged the Widow as she picked up her basket.

George led Widow Small to the front door, where she draped her shawl around her shoulders. He watched her slowly shuffle to the front gate. She stopped and turned around.

"It will seem strange not being here all the time."

"You're always welcome, Widow Small," called George waving to the old lady. He closed the door and leant against it. He sighed heavily and murmured.

"I just hope I've made the right decision."

George and Grace moved into Sullens within the week. The house was in dire need of a woman's touch again, being left unkempt since May's death. Grace began to bring the old house back to life again. As the summer months arrived, Sullens bloomed once more.

છ

Thomas Dove spent little time at Sullens now. His grief was still very apparent to the extent that he could hardly bring himself to hold his son, James. It brought back too many sad memories of May; to look into his eyes brought tears to his own. His time was now spent working at his business in Newport and lodging at the local Inn, *The Castle*, whiling away many wasted hours looking into glass upon glass of ale. He had made the acquaintance of a local girl, Elizabeth Loader who worked a short distance away from Thomas's business. He felt he had made a firm friend with whom he was able to confide in. Elizabeth was fully aware of Thomas' plight and she was able to take away some of the pain Thomas suffered. Their friendship blossomed through time into a fond love and the two decided to marry at the little church in Chawton village, a few miles from Newport.

Thomas decided to summon the Moreys to meet with him at Sullens to explain his intentions to marry Elizabeth. As the whole family sat around the parlour table, there was a deathly hush. Michal was the first to speak.

"What about the child? Are you taking him away with you?"

"I have come to the decision," said Thomas, "that it will be best for James to remain at Sullens. At a place that he has always known. I don't want to unsettle him by taking him away. I will of course ensure that he is well provided for and there will be a sum of money available when needed. There will also be funds held in a trust for him when he comes of age."

"Do you think that's wise for a child to be without both his natural parents?" asked Grace in amazement. She was unable to comprehend why Thomas felt the way he did about the boy.

"Grace, I know what is best for the child. You are more than qualified to care for him than I. He is growing into a fine child and settled here and he does not see much of me as it stands. A move to a new home and a new mother would only upset him. Besides, I believe

May always wanted him to be reared at Sullens." Thomas broke off and turned to look at towards Michal who was sat at the head of the table.

"How do you feel about the matter Michal?" He looked pensively at his father-in-law.

"It is your decision, Thomas. You know what you want in life. The child is welcome to stay, he's no trouble. Grace can manage; he is of no age to understand though. You will have to answer his questions when he's older. He is bound to ask why. I hope you have gall and honesty to tell him."

Michal was deeply disappointed in the way Thomas was dealing with the whole affair, not least that he was to marry again after what seemed a short time since May's death.

"I know. I have thought of that," said Thomas at length. He gauged the reaction of all sat around the table.

It was not a task that he was longing to carry out but he felt that the sooner he left Sullens and the memories, the sooner he could begin to lose his grief. James was the last reminder of May that he wanted to let go, once and for all.

"When will you leave, Thomas?" asked George.

"I have a date in mind, of April that we are to wed at Chawton," said Thomas, "so I will have my belongings taken from Sullens in the coming weeks."

"So be it," said Michal without looking up. "Have we any mead left, Grace? I have the thirst of twelve men!"

Thomas rose from the table. He sensed Michal wasn't particularly upset to learn of his leaving Sullens. After all, they had not forged a strong relationship since meeting for the first time. It was only May that kept them from arguing. He watched Michal gulp large quantities of mead in a short time and slam his glass onto the table demanding more from Grace like a spoilt child. He felt the day he would leave Sullens for good could not come soon enough.

CHAPTER NINE

"Where is Papa? Where has he gone?" Came the enquiring young voice of James Dove.

"He's gone away boy…gone away for a while," came Michal's well-rehearsed reply.

"Where….?" the piercing voice demanded.

"To far away lands, far away boy," replied Michal. His patience began to wane.

"Is he dead? Like mother; is he dead, is he?" James was beginning to irritate Michal and try his patience to the point of him wanting to issue the boy a clip behind his ear.

"No, he aint dead. Good lord child, so many questions," said Michal and glared at the boy.

"Whh…hhhy?" James was persistent with his questions throwing Michal into a quandary. He didn't want James to know too much at this stage about his father remarrying and living in Cowes.

"Look boy…" he pleaded in exasperation, "just leave me in peace, I need my rest."

"Why?" James looked at Michal in bewilderment.

"Because I am old and need my rest, now be off with you!" Michal pointed towards the house, and gestured with his hand for James to leave him alone. He rubbed his forehead; the boy was forever asking questions about Thomas. Michal had tried his best to settle the boy's curiosity but he had not overcome the demands James put upon him. He could hardly blame the boy. It was only natural he wanted to know where his father was. Michal felt it unfair to tell the boy that he only lived a few miles away on the Island. He feared the boy might try to go in search of him and, if he knew where his father lived would come to no good at all. Thomas had been left Sullens nearly eight years now and James was growing into a smart young boy. He attended school upon his father's passing request in Newport on a regular basis and the barrage of questions he received were as a result of the queries plied from his fellow class mates. James had to bear the brunt of endless teasing and he needed answers to the many questions he faced.

George and Grace were wonderful with James, they treated him like he was their own child knowing always how to humour the young steed and they brought him up to be a well behaved child. Widow Small continued to offer her generosity towards the Moreys. She enjoyed her frequent visits to Sullens and, on many occasions, she always bought James a small gift, of a toy or new clothes that she had tailored herself. James always referred to the Widow as Granny and considered her part of his own family. She often told James how special he was to her and remarked.

"You are a talented child, James! A true scholar! How lucky you are to have an education. There was none of that for the likes of me or your grandfather."

One day, Michal was sitting in the parlour room when he heard the Widow talk to James.

"You've certainly been given a better start haven't you young man? Golden boy; just like your father!" She cooed.

Michal shifted in his chair and thought of Thomas and his thriving business. He had reservations over James' ready-made wealth ably provided by his father. He resented the fact the boy had the chance to become wealthy without having to make an honest living. James would never have to labour amongst trees to earn his living. The boy, in his eyes was spoilt, with Thomas having provided a tidy sum before he left to ensure James' life was of good quality. Michal attention faded and he looked towards the kitchen, he felt hungry.

"Any food ready Grace, I'm hungry," he called out selfishly, not moving from his chair.

"It won't be long now," called Grace "by the way, my sister Ann will be joining us for dinner."

"Oh, is she…?" said Michal in surprise, "pretty girl that one!" he added with a sly grin.

Grace smiled. Michal seemed to spend his days in a dream. He was oblivious to the real world. He mostly spoke in short sentences or grunted every now and again. Grace had often confided in George over Michal's sanity. George reassured her that his father had lived through so much grief in his life, with the death of many of his family and it was his way of coping. He told Grace not to worry over him.

"He is old now, Grace. He's tired, just leave him be; he enjoys living that way now," said George, as he looked at the concern in Grace's eyes.

"Do you think he should give up working in the wood?" she asked.

"Should the sun stop shining?" asked George and his face broke into a grin. "That is the only thing that keeps him going. Once, he would have denied any love for that wood, but now, it seems to be his only solace, that and the cottage."

"Each to his own, I trust," said Grace. "Here, take this to the table, please. Ann will be here soon."

"Yes, my beloved," said George, kissing the top of Grace's head and taking the basket of bread to the parlour.

There was a soft knocking at the door and Grace called out to James to answer it.

"Go and let your Aunt Ann in please, James."

Ann stood on the doorstep; she was Grace's younger sister who was eighteen with brown hair tied in a single plait. Her bonnet was set at the back of her head. She was quite rotund for her years, unlike her sister who was tall and slim. She saw James coyly peering around the door and she boomed in a loud but very cheerful voice.

"Hello young James, how are you keeping?"

"Well thank you, Aunt Ann," said James withdrawing quickly from her open thrusting arms that tried to envelope his whole body in a loving crush. He ran into the parlour as Ann slowly followed waddling through the doorway.

"Hello my sweet heart, and how are you?" yelled Michal as he jumped up from the chair and ran towards the startled Ann. He grabbed her shoulders and planted a heavy kiss on her cheek.

"Granfer, I am well! How are you?" She looked at his drawn face and tried not to stare as she noticed how much Michal had aged since she last saw him. *Granfer* was her pet name for Michal as she found it difficult to call him by his first name.

"Well... fairing well, as usual..." His attention was drawn back to Grace who had brought the dinner to the table. James was standing in front of Michal when he blundered towards the food. Cursing as James was in the way, he yelled at him, "Get out of the way boy! Let the dog see the rabbit!"

He stumbled throwing himself on the nearest convenient chair and roared, "Where is it then Grace for God's sake? Are we to starve today?"

"Michal! Where are you manners?" Grace said angrily to him, "hush your noise, be patient for once in your life!"

"Me? Patient? Don't you mock me girl!" retorted Michal as he dragged his hand over his head to try to push hair from his eyes.

"James, be seated next to your Grandfather please," said Grace. She glanced at James and tried to keep herself from looking at Michal who sat glaring at her with a demonic stare.

"Come on boy," coaxed Michal "sooner you sit… sooner we're fed!"

Michal looked at Ann as she approached the table and sat opposite him, "And why pray are you quiet tonight, Ann?" He smiled at her baring his teeth in a sickly fashion.

"No reason Granfer, I'm listening to you and your noise!" Ann's remark made Michal suddenly realise how badly he was behaving. He sat back and composed himself.

"I'm sorry Ann, lost my manners somewhat. Don't take any notice; I'm just a silly old man."

He looked to Grace, she acknowledged the apology and they began to eat. The family sat in silence eating the fine meal of meat, bread and potatoes. Ann proceeded to idly chatter and gossip and soon the two sisters were ensconced in conversation. Michal intermittently roared with laughter even though he had no idea what they were talking about as he had drunk rather a lot of mead during the meal. George glared at his father and their eyes met. For much of the time he was able to tolerate Michal's behaviour, but as Ann was a guest, that they did not have the chance to see that often, he found Michal to be particularly irritating. At length when Michal's laughter became hysterical and James was clearly distressed by the antics of his grandfather, George decided to take action.

"Why don't you take a walk outside for a while father, check on the cottage, you have not been there for a while," George suggested in the hope Michal would take the bait.

"You are right boy, I need some air. I'll go now. Must make sure its still standing!" said Michal.

He staggered to his feet. After he had left, George heaved a huge sigh of relief.

"Ann, please don't listen to the old man. He can be full of demons some days, well… most days, but it's just the drink. I am sorry for what he said tonight."

"Don't you worry George, I understand, after all, he has suffered in the past, it's not been easy for him." Ann smiled at her brother-in-law. She was a very understanding girl. Michal didn't frighten her at all in company. She felt confident when she was not alone with him as she felt she had other members of the family to back her up, however being faced alone with him would be a situation she would rather never experience.

As the evening wore on and Grace had put James to bed, George became concerned that Michal had not returned to Sullens yet. He glanced at Grace.

"Father has been a long time, must be a good couple of hours since he left."

"Do you think we should look for him?" asked Grace.

Suddenly they heard James call out, "Where is grandfather?"

"Grace hurried to the bottom of the stairs, "James, hush now go back to sleep, grandfather is at his cottage, he'll be back soon."

"Can I look for him?" he asked sleepily.

"No, grandfather forgets the time when he is there," soothed Grace.

"Do you think he is talking to…them?" asked James as he began to feel afraid of the thoughts of the lost souls his grandfather often told him of that lurked within the four walls of the cottage.

Grace then realised what he was talking about.

"No, there are no such things," She looked alarmed and wondered just what Michal had been telling the boy.

Ann joined in.

"There are no such things; that is the truth James. I know that because Widow Small told me years ago. She does not believe, and she told *me* not to either," she reassured him.

"Ghosts are real. Grandfather told me so, he told me of them at the cottage," James' voice quivered in fear and Grace hurried upstairs to comfort him.

"Stop your talk now James, you'll have bad dreams," she led him back to his bed.

"I'm not afraid Aunt Grace, really I'm not." James tried to be brave. Grace held him close to her. As she cuddled his little frame, she thought how much he had to learn about life. She didn't want to worry him unnecessarily but she felt angered that Michal was poisoning his own grandson's mind at such a tender age.

George called up the stairs.

"I'm going out to look for father, he must have fallen asleep there; I will be back soon."

He left Sullens just as rain had begun to pelt down. Grace wished he hadn't gone; why couldn't Michal be left to his own fate? She felt that George cared too much for the old man, more than he ever deserved. As he neared the cottage, George could just see the outline of Michal wandering aimlessly from one side of the lane to the other.

He called out.

"Father! What are you doing?"

"I've lost her; she was here just a while ago... now she'd hiding from me!" Michal's speech was slurred and he reeked of alcohol swaying as he spoke.

"Come back to Sullens father, perhaps she is there!" said George as the rain beat heavily against his face. He realised he was talking about Beth.

"Yes, she might be there, you may be right boy, she'll be in the garden as usual," Michal pushed past George and stumbled in the direction of Sullens.

The rain had drenched his body and his hair was soaked in layers matted like rats tails, but he didn't seem to notice as he blundered off into the darkness leaving George standing alone. He called out into the distance.

"There you are you! Bad girl, come on Beth, get back in the house, you know you'll get sick if you stay out in this rain!"

George heard Michal fall heavily to the ground. He ran and helped the old man to his feet and guided him back home. The lantern at the front door at Sullens swayed back and forth amidst the storm. George opened the door and led Michal into the warmth; the brightness of the light hurt their eyes. Michal squinted and stopped in his tracks exclaiming in a loud voice.

"But… but she's *not* here!" He glanced around in dismay and looked at George.

"You told me she would be *here*! You *lied* to me boy, you know what I say to *liars* don't you?"

"Come on father, let's get you upstairs, go to your bed, you need rest." George pulled Michal towards the stairs.

"Not till I've found Beth!" screamed Michal pulling away from George's grasp and heading back to the front door again.

"For god's sake Michal, you are scaring the boy!" yelled Grace as she ran into the hall where George struggled to keep hold of his drunken father.

"Leave it be! She's gone! Don't you understand? Beth is dead. She has been for years now. She is not here!

She…is…dead!" screamed Grace hysterically. She wrung her hands in front of her. She turned away from Michal for fear she would hit him.

"What's wrong with *her*?" asked Michal in surprise, he looked puzzled by Grace's outburst.

"Father, upstairs now!" ordered George shoving Michal forward, he held his collar firmly as he urged the old man up the stairs.

Grace walked slowly back to the parlour, tears filled her eyes as Ann comforted her, placing an arm round her shoulders. James appeared from behind the door, he had quietly crept downstairs during the commotion. He sat silently at Grace's feet frightened that his grandfather, an adult, had seemed to have gone insane. He adored his grandfather and looked upon him as his father figure in place of his real father, Thomas.

"James, why don't you get Aunt Grace some water from the jug on the table, there's a good boy, go now," Ann urged the boy to his feet.

She looked at Grace who sobbed openly into her shoulder.

"Do you want me to stay for the night? Would it help for me to stay?"

"Yes, would you mind Annie? I've had enough of… that…old fool. I cannot understand how George is *so* patient with him. Now I am wondering about my own sanity!"

Grace wiped her tear stained face and took the glass of water from James who returned to his place at her feet.

"You're not mad, Grace. You aren't to blame for Michal's state of mind, no one is. It all happened over a long time. He just won't let go of the past, it has affected him and the drink that has poisoned his mind has not helped," Ann soothed.

Grace held on to Ann's hand and spoke silently.

"You are a good sister to me, Ann. I don't know how Widow Small put up with all this mess," Grace dried her eyes and tried to smile. James jumped to his feet and stared at Grace.

"Do you mean me? Am I...the mess?" he asked innocently.

"Of course not my lamb, of course not," Grace looked pitifully at James and pulled him towards her. He brushed aside her embrace and ran to the door, "I'm going to my bed!" he snivelled.

"James, dear!" cried Grace and ran after him but the boy slammed the door in her face.

Ann called out.

"Leave him be, Grace. He needs time to be alone, he'll cry a bit but he will be all right."

George was just closing the bedroom door behind Michal. As he turned round James ran past him into his bedroom sobbing. Grace had ignored Ann's advice and ran after him.

"What's wrong with the boy?" asked George.

"This place... his father...him in there!" cried Grace outraged pointing towards Michal.

She opened James' door and closed it gently behind her. From outside George could hear her talking to James, reassuring her love for him trying to explain. He heard James sobs that echoed around the whole upstairs of the house and it haunted him to his heart. He heard Ann calling from downstairs.

"George! Is everything all right?"

"Yes, fine Ann, don't worry, Grace is with the boy now." He returned downstairs to the parlour.

"Just a misunderstanding between James and Grace," George stood at the hearth his mind turning over and over.

"Seems like it's all a misunderstanding in this place!" sighed Ann. "How is Michal?" She felt it was time to probe George.

"Drunk...old, miserable, but asleep now. He'll probably awaken to a raging headache in the morn. No more than he deserves," replied George. He was completely ashamed at his father's performance that evening.

"I'll clear the table and tidy the kitchen," said Ann and she began to busy herself by collecting up spent crockery.

"I'll call it a night now; I will see you in the morning Ann and thank you for your help. Grace is glad you are staying tonight. She needs support now," said George.

"See you in the morrow, George. Try to rest as you never know when Granfer will stir," warned Ann, as she did so she saw the fatigue in George's eyes and the trouble he carried upon his shoulders.

CHAPTER TEN

Michal woke the next morning to a sharp, piercing pain, throbbing uncontrollably in his head. He carefully turned over in his bed and groaned like an angry bear disturbed from its sleep. He held his head in his hands as he lay helpless. He questioned himself aloud.

"Why do I do it?"

Rubbing his eyes, he tried to focus on the floor, but everything was in a haze and swam before his eyes. His room was unusually bright as the sun was shining quite high in the sky indicating it was well into mid-morning. Michal suddenly realised that he was late for work. He staggered awkwardly to his feet and tried to walk in a straight line, only to find himself falling about landing heavily on the floor. His body was sapped of energy and he felt extremely sick.

"Must be… cos I'm getting old, can't take with the ale. Mores the pity for sure, still it shan't stop me suppin," he grumbled openly to himself, as he battled to fasten his boots in a painful fashion.

Grace had made the decision that it would be better for Michal to remain asleep, to help rid him of the evil demons in his head so, when she left for town earlier that morning, she left the old man sleeping very soundly. Michal eventually stood and balanced himself and walked toward the window. He threw open the threadbare curtains and the bright light of the sun tormented his eyes. He screwed his eyes tightly and saw James in the field below playing, with Ann alongside watching over him. Michal dragged on his clothes that still reeked of the alcohol of the night before. He felt weak, weary and very tired, more than usual and his mood was not favourable. He stumbled down the stairs into the kitchen and through the open window to Ann in the garden he called, "I'll be at the wood, back later on."

James looked up and waved.

"Goodbye grandfather!" He had forgotten temporarily the drunken outburst from his grandfather the night before and treated Michal as he always did, with admiration. Ann smiled wryly at the old man as she watched him walk towards the wood. She didn't trust his mood that day, particularly when he was suffering with a hangover.

❧

Throughout the rest of the morning, Michal's mood did not improve, his work suffered from this consequence, as it did so very much of late. The Squire had made comment only the week before that Michal's work was poor and that he had to watch his step or he would be forced to rethink Michal's employ. Michal had remembered that remark with revenge and began to blindly clear some fallen boughs, trying to give an impression that he had been hard at work since early morning. As he began to pull on a large piece he caught his foot awkwardly and he fell unceremoniously to the ground. As he tried to get up every bone in his body ached and his head felt like it was splitting into tiny fragments like that of timber as an axe cut through it. He slowly got up and continued to amble around the copse; gone was the strong, sprightly woodcutter, now stood a tired old man, longing for permanent rest. However, Michal was a stubborn man and no way could he imagine not being in the wood. He had toiled there all his working life and he refused, as much as he could, to be replaced by a younger man. He must have been in a complete daze as the sudden appearance of young James made him jump up with a start.

"Good lord, boy! Where did you come from? What are you doing here in the wood?" he asked in unrehearsed surprise as he was taken aback to see James standing quietly behind him, looking up with an impish grin. James stood with this arms folded firmly in front of his chest. He smirked his reply.

"I was fed up with Ann, she is boring and fat!" came the cheeky reply as James kicked idly at a piece of wood lying near to his feet.

"That aint the way to talk of your Aunt boy…don't you talk bout her that way!"

∞

Michal was surprised by how rude James was talking of Ann. It was totally out of his normally reserved and well-behaved character. He could not think why the boy was acting so strangely. Michal stood upright and then leant forward on his axe handle, propping himself up on it. His head ached and this outburst from James was not helping.

"I do not care…she *is* fat," remarked James kicking again at the wood. Michal felt irritated by the boy's insolence and his rude manners. He began to frown at James; he felt an anger begin to well deep inside, making him lose his grip on the axe. It fell to the ground, the blade just visible in the long grass.

"You cannot judge folk like that, not cos of her size. What has she done to you to make you call her names?" Michal asked and picked up his axe, meticulously wiping the blade on his leggings, making the steel glisten once more.

"*Yes* I can! I can tell *anyone* what I think of them. I'm not taking orders from no-one!" James stood in defiance before the old man, hands on hips, he stood his ground.

He was in danger of seriously dabbling with Michal's already frayed patience.

"Don't talk that way James. You ain't got no right to talk that way! Is that what they learn you at that school... to talk badly of folk?" Michal felt his temper begin to boil as the boy cheekily addressed him again.

"Where is my father, *Michal?*" James suddenly demanded; his voice, shrill like a blackbird. He started to parade around the woodcutter taking large, meaningful steps. His arms still folded tight against his chest. His face was still wearing its uncharacteristic smirk.

Michal was amazed at being called by his Christian name especially by a child. He paused and leant on his axe using it like a walking stick.

"He is far away boy, like I told you before, far away."

"How far? How far *is* far away *Michal?*" James was thoroughly enjoying the confrontation and his confidence with the old man rapidly increased with each question posed. He started to walk briskly around the old man, taunting him with his questions, making leering gestures by poking out his tongue, "Tell me *Michal*, tell me now, I say!" he scoffed. His behaviour was deplorable...

"You call me *Grandfather*, not by my first name, understand me?" spluttered Michal in exasperation; he felt his grip suddenly tighten on the axe handle. The wood felt very solid in his grasp, its shaft undaunted.

"You have *not* told me *where* my father lives?" James stood with his hands on his hips defiantly, his legs astride amongst the grass. He looked extremely menacing for a young boy, but only the truth would satisfy this outburst of undoubted curiosity.

"I spose you should know, you're old enough now. Your father, Thomas, lives in Cowes," Michal eventually announced, the axe continued to swing by his side in rhythmic motions.

James stood and frowned; he thought for a while and then said.

"He is living in *Cowes*? How can *that* be? That is not *far* away! Why do you *always* tell me *far* away?"

Michal looked at the boy wishing he would stop questioning and said quietly.

"Because he married again… another woman, decided to leave you at Sullens to grow up. He did not want you, that's why he went, cos you reminded him of your mother, God bless her. He loved her very much, but…he didn't want *you* though. Couldn't bear to look at *you*, too many memories I 'spose, I don't know. All I know is we brought you up, me, Grace, the Widow, we was left to do it, we had to, see."

James became incensed.

"How *dare* he leave me!" He was close to tears but he remained as calm as he was able, he continued, "How dare he leave me with a tired, drunken old man and a silly fat Aunt!"

Michal lunged towards James. He was now dangerously out of control.

"How *dare* you… you little *bastard*! Say you're sorry! How *dare* you talk of your family, of the ones that brought you up when your father went away! Say you are sorry you beggar! Do you *hear* me?" Michal's face was very close against the boy, he glared hard into James' eyes, his face fixed, his teeth clenched in a menacing snarl.

"*Never*! I *hate* you all, all of you! Even Grace!" yelled James and he struggled away from Michal's grip, confused and devastated that his Father left on those terms. His questions were now finally answered. He felt he needed to escape, to have time to think it over, be alone, sulk, cry, anything that his emotions would throw at him.

"Say you're sorry or I'll see to you!" warned Michal, the blade on the axe glinted sharply against the sunlight, creating a brief flash. He maintained his grip as he balanced the axe high over his shoulder. Michal soon caught up with James and tried to lunge toward him. He spun the boy around, the strength of ten men had returned to those tired old bones, the rage of a man tormented to the extreme, the strong emotions of a man plagued by tragedy throughout most of his life, the anger of a man who had a point to put across to a young boy who had scorned his own family. The people who cared for him. Who had brought him up, given him a life that he may not have had with his father.

James stupidly taunted him once again.

"I *never* will, you drunken old fool, and I hate you! I *hate all* of you…I especially ha...... ughhhh!"

187

Michal had risen high up above the boy like a demon possessed and wielded his axe in a stance of attack, its blade flashed like lightning as he brought it down hard, plunging it deep into James' chest. James dropped to the earth like a stone. Again and again Michal hacked at the boy; blood spurted from the gashes in all directions as the axe bit deeper into his flesh, deep into the now silent and lifeless body of James Dove.

Michal threw the axe to the ground as though it had burnt his hands. He shook in fear. He fell to his knees beside James' body. He opened his mouth and tried to scream but no sound was heard. Blood lay spattered in the grass like a shroud of death that surrounded the body. His eyes were transfixed to the boy, shocked at his outburst, he couldn't breath. He rocked in slow motion to and fro, to and fro waiting to see James breathe, but there was no breath. Life had been sucked completely from the little boy and he had been the one to take it from him. He had sacrificed a life for the sake of words and opinion. Words that had hurt the woodcutter; upset him. *Only* words, nothing more. Something that could have been avoided, had he'd accepted the boy's accusations. He looked at the blood that had soaked the grass around him. He looked at the blade that dripped crimson against cold steel. The blade that he had used to slay a child. Michal stared in stupefied horror at the body that lay still, with so many wounds inflicted upon it that he could no longer make out its proportional shape. He turned away closing his eyes briefly before being violently sick. His head pulsated so rapidly causing him to wince in pain. He held his head in his heads and began to cry in desperation.

The boy had pushed Michal too far, far beyond his limitation but as he stood a few feet away from the mangled body, Michal could not comprehend that he could commit such an act, an act of murder. The murder of his own grandson; his daughter's boy, dear May, his *own* kin. Panic set into Michal's mind as he backed away from the body. He tried to compose himself but his whole body shook with uncontrollable, erratic fear. He sank back to his knees as once more his legs refused to work. For the first time since Mary's death he prayed openly to God, for forgiveness of his evil deed.

"Please God, look at me, *please* don't punish me, not any more. I did it…I know I did, I…just…couldn't…." He broke off, his voice strangled in grief. As he sat alone in the wood with the body of James lying a few feet away, the whole wood was eerily quiet as if it had been shaken by the terrible event it had just witnessed. He looked skyward and whispered.

"Beth, why do you *just* watch, can't you help me, help me, just help me………"

All around Michal, nothing except the untimely death of a young boy who, only a few moments ago was alive and in his prime of youth had altered. The brief silence had now passed and the birds had started their merry chatter once more. Fear struck Michal like a stone; he wondered what he should do now. Should he tell anyone of this nightmare?

Could he entrust his son George with his guilt? No, he felt it best to keep this horror to himself; his conscience warned him to say nothing, to tell no one. *"Get rid of it, get rid of it!"* he heard the voices inside his head chant.

"But where?" he asked aloud looking fearfully about him. He imagined faces looking at the murder scene, of being discovered. He thought wildly, trying to compose himself. He suddenly remembered the leather panniers that he used to carry wood. He got up quickly and walked towards the body.

He stopped instantly.

"I can't do this, I need to tell someone. I...can't...."

He began to weep hysterically again as he tried to drag the body into the pannier. His own clothing soon became soaked in James blood. It was warm and sticky to the touch and Michal tried to wipe it frantically from his clothes to rid the evidence, but only made it worse and soon he was completely covered in it. Guilty, not only in the mind, but visually too. He wore the clothes of a murderer.

Rooks circled round the tops of the trees like vultures, cackling and mocking the murderous woodcutter far down below their flight, amongst the trees amid a river of blood. They were the eye-witnesses to this evil act. Michal awkwardly tied the pannier with fingers fumbling so badly. He made several attempts to fasten its grisly cargo, to encase the body from view and began to drag it from the wood, leaving a trail of blood as he did so. He tried to hoist it over his shoulder but the weight was too much for his frame, even though it was only the weight of a child. He had to hide the body quickly before anyone saw him and became suspicious. He arrived back at the entrance to the lane. He saw his cottage a few yards away, he didn't have far to go now. He glanced quickly up and down the lane to make sure no one was there.

'Good, deserted,' he said to himself as he dragged the body across the lane close to the hedgerow looking all about him at each step. His imagination ran riot throughout his mind as he heard imaginary hoof beats and the sound of voices.

Michal reached the cottage and heaved the body through the tiny doorway, into the passage to the kitchen where he placed it roughly under the stairs in the darkest corner. Exhausted, he sank to the floor, still crying, unable to control his grief. Grief not only for young James but for the rest of his dead relatives he had lost before. He wept for his son George, for Grace, for Thomas Dove as he thought how this tragedy would ruin their lives. He thought of the Widow Small, wailing in horror as she learned the news and finally, he wept for his own fate and what would befall him. He thought of the hue and cry that would no doubt shortly follow his disappearance and of the mob that would be searching for him. Michal knew he had to get away and soon.

The cottage was cloaked in a deathly hush, no bird song, no light and no air. The kitchen remained shadowed like a shrine to the dead boy and smelt strongly of dampness and neglect.

After a long while, Michal dragged himself to his feet. He stumbled through the dark to the fire and dragged a stick through the dying embers causing a few brief sparks to flicker into life. Suddenly, he found himself dragging those embers onto the kitchen floor. He began to paw furiously at them, spreading the hot coals. He kicked them frantically with his boots. The embers quickly licked up strands of dusty straw, which lay on the wooden floor. The embers grew to smoke, then to small jets of flames that crackled as they increased in intensity. Michal feverishly threw any object he could find onto the flames as the fire took hold. He backed away from the now scorching heat as the flames reached James' body under the stairs and began to engulf it. Glancing about him, Michal found a piece of dry bread and a blanket and fled from the cottage, slamming the door behind him. He ran in a staggered frenzy back towards the wood as the light was beginning to fade from the sky. He knew of a cave used by an old hermit some years back that was close to the clearing in the wood. He could stay there initially and decide what next to do. He felt this would be the only place he could hide away from sight, away from the people who would soon be hunting for him, the murderer, away from the militia that no doubt would be called to search for him, the dogs and their hunger for flesh.   He continued to hurry as best he could away from the cottage, he could smell the air was beginning to fill with the smell of pungent smoke. He looked back and saw flames leaping high above the thatched roof of the cottage, which was now completely ablaze.

At Sullens, Grace had returned and found Ann sewing in the parlour, alone in the house.

"Hello Ann, where is James?" she asked casually.

Ann looked up.

"I thought he was with you!" she exclaimed as her heart began to beat faster. "He told me no more than a couple of hours since that he was going to meet you along Coach Lane!"

"Well, I've not seen him. Oh well, I expect he's found Michal at the wood. He'll soon be back, when he feels the need for food," sighed Grace untying the ribbons to her bonnet from under her chin. She placed her basket on the table then stood still and listened.

"Grace," said Ann. "Can you hear something? Like a crackling noise? It can't be Michal can it? He should be finished work by now, lest he has extra errands from the Squire."

"Yes, I hear the noise," said Grace as she stood still and continued to listen hard.

"It sounds like gun fire. Oh my lord!" she suddenly cried as she caught sight of billowing smoke through the kitchen window. She looked at Ann.

"It's the cottage, its on fire!   Quick, raise the neighbours, I'm going straight there!"

Grace ran down the lane to Michal's cottage, which was blazing out of control. The smoke had blotted out what remained of the daylight. At a safe distance there stood a few villagers who had gathered when they saw the smoke. They had formed a human chain and were passing buckets of water from the nearby well to the fire, desperately throwing them, trying to fight back the flames. Grace ran up to the nearest person, grabbing their arm she yelled,

"Where is Michal, have you seen Michal? Has *anyone* seen him?"

"No one has seen him missus, but they think he may be inside the place!" One of the villagers panted, as he continued to receive buckets of water.

"Oh my God, please help me, someone help, can they not get inside? Dear God!" Grace became hysterical and burst into sobs of tears. Ann had eventually reached the scene, puffing heavily, her face red with exhaustion of having to run up the lane. She comforted Grace and held her tightly.

"George has been sent for, he'll be on his way I'm told!" she said to Grace.

"Where is James, why did he disobey you? Where *is* Michal?" wailed Grace. She felt nauseous with the stench of the swirling smoke and burning thatch.

"No one has seen either of them. Shall I go back to Sullens to see if the boy has returned there?" Ann asked looking terrified at her sister.

"No, stay here please, Ann. I have a terrible thought that something has happened and they are, that they are both ...." she broke off into sobs.

"Steady Grace, pray to God you're feelings are wrong... that they are both safe," said Ann trying to soothe her sister's worse fears. Deep down she felt herself that the news would not be good, but she prayed somehow she would be wrong.

⌘

Michal drew the blanket tightly up to his chin. He had begun to shiver all over and the cave was very damp and uninviting. James' blood was still damp upon his clothing and the stench of death haunted him. He tried shutting his eyes but every time he did so he saw James' stricken face as Michal raised the axe to butcher him. He heard the boy taunting him, then stop as his body fell to the floor with the axe deep in the boy's chest. He then saw the lifeless corpse lying in the grass covered in blood. Covering his face with his bloodstained and smoke drenched hands, Michal tried to block the nightmares from his mind. He asked himself many times why? Why had he murdered the boy? Beth had always warned him that his temper could one day kill. How right she was. He tried to summon her through his mind but without success.

"Beth, please... help me, help your stupid... drunken, murderer of a husband, help me in this terrible hour!"

He looked into the darkness in earnest hoping to see or hear Beth. The only voices he heard were shouts in the distance. He froze, listening hard, not daring to breathe. "They must be at the cottage," he thought aloud, as he looked toward the noise he could see the orangey glow of the fire in the distance. The fire at the cottage that he had started and the many people there who were trying to put it out. The cave was in pitch black now as the sun had finally set causing the temperature to plummet. The smell of musty, decaying undergrowth sickened Michal to the pit of his stomach. He wondered how long it would be before someone raised the alarm that James was missing. He gripped hold of his knees as his thoughts returned to his crime. He was now labelled as a murderer, and would be hunted for the killing of James Dove.

ح‌٤

As the fire subsided, the villagers were able to start searching the shell of the cottage. It had taken most of the night to extinguish it and the nearby well was depleted of all its contents. George held Grace close to him as there was a shout from one of the men folk.

"There's a body in the kitchen, not much left of it though, looks like a young 'un. I need some help; someone lend a hand I ask you!"

Grace gripped hold of George's hand until he felt she might crush it.

"Tell me it's not James, tell me please! It's not the little boy!"

"We do not know. It could be another; it could be a stranger using it as a doss house. Father doesn't use it that much does he?"

"No, but he's there more times than we know. Where *is* he by the way?" asked Grace suddenly.

"Oh back at Sullens drinking himself stupid there is no doubt of that. I don't know how we will break the news about the cottage to him. It meant everything to him."

George stopped talking as the two men appeared from behind the wreckage of the cottage dragging a body behind them. George immediately left Grace's side and walked quickly towards them, leaving Grace to cling to Ann. The two women stood with their breath baited. George slowly returned to them and quietly announced.

"They are taking the body to St George's, we have been told to meet the Doctor there; we are to go now. The body...," George hesitated and cleared his throat, "the body...is possibly that of... James."

Grace swooned and fell to the ground like a stone. Ann bent down to her aid, tears welling in her eyes. George helped Grace to her feet and into a horse and cart that had come from the village and would take them to the church. They were driven away to the village in silence. The Doctor was already waiting for their arrival. The body had been transported in a separate cart just moments before. The Doctor looked very grave.

"I have not checked the body," he said. "This is a sorry affair, a dreadful business. Does anyone know how all this happened?" He looked directly at George and Grace.

"Only that the cottage was ablaze and James may have been inside at the time. We thought he was with Michal when he did not turn up to meet Grace along Coach Lane," said George solemnly.

"Does anyone know where Michal is?" asked the Doctor quietly.

"He's not been seen since he left for the wood this morning. One of the Squire's men went to look for him but he's not there. It seemed strange, they found his axe near the wood pile, yet it was too dark to see if there was any other sign of Michal having been there. He never leaves that thing anywhere. I think he'll be back at Sullens now. I just dread having to tell him about the cottage…and…that…," said George, his mind was racing trying to fathom exactly what had occurred.

"George, would you please follow me to the vestry, I need you see the body and tell me who you think it is. Pardon me, Grace, but I will not put you through this ordeal. Please wait here until we return."

As they entered the vestry, the smell of smoke filled the tiny room; the doctor led George to a table where the body lay. He turned slowly and faced George.

"I have been informed… that the body was… encased inside a leather pannier. Do you think… the boy may have been playing at the cottage? Hiding perhaps and fell asleep?"

"I have never known James to go to the cottage alone. He was always too scared. The place was haunted according to father and this always scared the boy enough not to go near it," said George, remembering the night when James had told of the ghosts at the cottage.

"Tis a very sorry affair," said the Doctor. "I am sorry you have to be the one to witness this tragedy. I have summoned for Thomas Dove but learn that he is away on business. What news to tell a father of his son! George, please look at the body, take a good look, beyond the burns and tell me who you see."

The doctor led George to the body. Together they carefully opened the smouldering pannier with iron hooks to protect their hands, as much heat was still generating from it. As they stood close to it George gulped in horror when he saw the charred and chopped human remains of first the feet and legs, then the torso and finally the face, which was unmistakably that of James Dove. George turned away quickly from the body. His stomach heaved and he held his hand hard against his mouth. He drew breath and staggered backwards, his eyes unable to comprehend the sight that would eventually haunted him for the rest of his life.

"Yes...doctor, that...is...James Dove....ugh!" He broke down. The doctor steadied George. He looked back at the corpse and swallowed slowly. He gently replaced the pannier to hide the remains.

"God rest his soul, poor dear child. What in God's name has happened to him?" George asked the Doctor, looking for a reason or explanation as he couldn't comprehend what he had just witnessed.

"Come George, away from here; go back to Sullens, get Grace home and wait for me there. I have to carry out some investigations and arrange for the undertaker Hance to collect the body. I will be with you in God's speed. Go now George, look after Grace and Ann."

The Doctor ushered George from the vestry, far away from the stench of the burnt corpse.

George took hold of Grace's hand when they were reunited. She was standing at the church gate and as they left the church together, the cry of despair from Grace could be heard throughout Arreton as far away as the cave where Michal lay in hiding. The bloodcurdling cry pierced right through his troubled mind. Michal closed his eyes tightly and slammed his hands over his ears. He started to shake. Grace's fears had been confirmed. James was dead!

CHAPTER ELEVEN

George closed the bedroom door quietly, so as not to wake Grace. It had taken hours for her to settle down to a troubled sleep and he did not wish to wake her as he left the room. He met Ann at the top of the stairs.

"Its all right, she's drifted off to sleep at last. I never thought she would though," he whispered raising a finger to his mouth.

"Oh George!" sighed Ann quietly. "This has to be a dream, all of it; I cannot believe this could happen!" She leant against the wall for support and closed her eyes. It was late into the night as the stricken family tried to get some rest after the day's tragedy.

"I wonder where on *earth* father is?" said George trying to look to Ann for answers. "The longer he's gone the more I am convinced he has had some part in this. He *has* to be involved somehow," he continued.

"Granfer will look after himself. You know what he can be like, George. He may be blind drunk lying in the wood somewhere, he'll wake and have the sense to come back to Sullens," reassured Ann. "But, he *has* to be told of James. It has to be *soon*," she added, looking towards George she noticed how concerned he was.

"I do wonder. I know father's moods and his way of thinking. I saw him look at James sometimes; there was jealousy in his eyes. He could never understand why the boy did not want for anything, how he had the chance to enjoy his childhood. I believe father *is* involved," said George sadly and he looked bleakly towards the floor.

Ann gasped in horror, realisation overcoming her mind.

"Oh my lord! Do you think he may have *killed* James?"

"I just don't know Ann. The doctor said earlier, he was concerned about wounds on the body, which were difficult to make out in the charred remains. He said he was sure it looked as if the boy had been stabbed by a knife or blade of sorts, some wounds were of a considerable size."

Ann froze in horror and gripped George's arm.

"Axe wounds?" she hesitated, her mind instantly flashed back to James playing in the morning. "Do you think James went to the wood to find Michal instead of meeting Grace? Do you suppose he met Michal and..." her voice trailed off in horror.

"Yes…yes it… could be," came the slow response from George. He closed his eyes and placed his hands to his head.

"I know James was in a strange mood this morning. He kept on telling me that I was fat and how he thought his grandfather was a drunken old fool. I can't think what made him talk that way. Perhaps it was because of what happened the night before. He did become restless and said he was going to meet Grace along the lane. I told him to be careful and make sure that if he did not see her to return back to Sullens straight away, but he must have gone to the wood instead." Ann tried to remember everything that happened that morning and as she retold it to George, the more she said the more everything fell into place.

"It seems to be what when on," said George, his mind was playing over and over. He was exhausted both mentally and physically. Ann touched his hand.

"You *too* need rest George. Go, be with Grace, try to sleep, perhaps there will be news of Michal in the morn, there is nothing you can do now."

"Yes, goodnight Ann, God bless you," George smiled weakly at her, keeping a brave face.

One person was not sleeping at all that night. Richard Norris stared out of his window at the dead of night, looking to the sky. He could smell the charred wood and smoke that penetrated down through the village as the wind was blowing in the direction of Arreton. He was thinking, long and hard. He remembered one of the day's he had met Beth outside the cottage and how she had enticed him into the place. He thought of how they had kissed each other and how they had declared their love for one another. Richard also remembered saying, after Beth's death, how he would one day ensure he would get his revenge upon Michal. As he stood by the window, he realised that this day had now come and that revenge would soon be met upon the man who had stolen Beth from him. He ran his fingers through his hair and walked away from the window. He sat heavily down upon the parlour chair and planned his next move.

Richard would normally have made his weekly pilgrimage toward Newport in the morning; but this would have to be delayed, as tomorrow he would be arranging a meeting of the local people. This meeting would be to form a group. A group who would be involved in a man hunt. The hunt for a murderer in their midst. He closed his eyes and thought of Michal Morey. His disappearance was oddly coincidental. The cottage burnt to the ground, a smouldering wreck. The body of a child, James Dove discovered within its ruins, encased in a leather pannier, frequently used by the woodcutter. The evidence was stacked against Morey and Richard was only too aware of this factor. He knew he had to act and quickly. He had a point to prove and time was short.

ᘎ

The next morning he addressed the impatient crowd.

ᘎ

"Well, Norris. When do we leave?" Yelled a voice from the back of the room. There were at least twenty local people crammed into Richard Norris' parlour, all poised to start the manhunt.

"Soon, Ned," Richard announced. "We know that Morey aint been seen for two days, not since the fire. Not since young James Dove was found, hacked to death and burnt. Don't you think it's strange, he aint been seen? Why do you think that is then? Shall I tell ya? It's because he is a *murderer*. A stinking, murdering coward, that's taken off somewhere. But, he aint gonna be that far, he aint got the sense to run far. He's old; he's running scared. So I say, let us go, *now*! Find this murdering bastard! Get him strung up in the gallows. The hue and cry starts *now*!" Richard shouted, whisking the mob into a frenzy, making them wave whatever they held in their hands, be it sticks, or farming implements. They were ready for a hunt and ready to catch the murderer.

The crowd roared as Richard defiantly led them out of his cottage and on towards Coach Lane. They yelled as they made their way, thumping their sticks to the ground in time as they chanted, "*Morey, Morey, Morey…*"

The mob walked in long and meaningful strides. Their chatter was frenzied and fast as they marched. They soon reached the edge of Pan Wood; Richard stopped and turned to address the group.

"Right. Pay your respects if you feel you want to," he said pointing towards the remains of the cottage. "When you're done, start looking in the wood. I tell you he won't be far. I'm going to Sullens and find the rest of his family and talk to them. Perhaps *they* know where Morey is hiding!"

The mob simultaneously cheered and split up in the direction of the wood, beating at the foliage as they bellowed out their chants of "*Murderer*". Some had taken dogs with them, which they had released from their leashes and were loose, baying for their intended prey.

Richard walked on with the remaining members of the mob towards Sullens. He wanted answers to the many questions folk were asking.

He saw George Morey standing at the doorway of the house. The look of concern on his face made Richard more determined. He walked straight up to George.

"Where is your father?" He demanded. His face inches from George's.

"I don't know, Richard. He aint here, that's for sure," George replied looking at the rest of the mob that were stood a few feet away, some handling their sticks in a warrior like fashion.

"We want to know where he *is*," Richard continued to demand. He reached and held George's collar stiffly in his hands.

"If I knew, I would tell you, believe me. He aint been seen," George responded; his voice was very quiet and calm.

"So, you don't care if we look for *ourselves* then?" Richard hissed, still holding onto George's collar.

"Look if you want, there aint nothin to see," George replied. "Just remember, there's women folk in there, they are still grieving, like me....we all lost the boy... think of that!"

Richard released his hold on George's collar and pushed him away. He indicated for the mob to start searching the house and the grounds for any sign of Michal. They began to beat their way through undergrowth and search the barns for the missing woodcutter. George made his way into the house. He called out to Grace and Ann.

"There's a mob searching for father, they want to see if he's here," he shouted.

Grace and Ann clung to each other in terror in the hallway as five men pushed past them into the house, over turning chairs and the table as they swept through Sullens. Grace called out to George.

"Stop them, George, stop them!" she pleaded.

"They won't go till they know he aint here," was the response from George who stood looking shocked in the garden, watching the mob relentlessly search for a man that wasn't there.

Grace looked at Richard Norris.

"I hope you're satisfied, Norris. Who in God's name do you *think* you are? The Militia?"

"No, I don't, Grace. But rest assured, they have been told of this. It won't be long now before they'll be here!" Richard replied standing with his arms folded, feet apart.

"How do you think *we* feel? James is *dead*! We don't know if he was murdered, we don't know that it wasn't him who started the fire there. How can you judge a man without knowing everything?"

"Morey is guilty. Mark my words, Morey *is* guilty," Richard said adamantly, as he spoke he stared straight at Grace.

"Get out of our house! Get out you crazed idiots!" Ann stood in the doorway brandishing a broom.

Richard acknowledged Ann's presence by bowing low in mock fashion.

"As you please, young Ann. As you please. Remember, he aint good, he's evil and he will pay for this!" He uttered through gritted teeth. He beckoned to the mob to follow him.

"Come, there's no sign of him here. Let's away to the wood, join the rest. We'll get him! We'll get him!"

Richard marched away from Sullens leaving the Morey family shaken and dreadfully upset. George stalked back into the parlour, picking up spent pieces of furniture and trying to put them back in their respective positions.

"What do they *mean*, George? Do they know something we don't?" asked Grace in despair.

"It don't look good, Grace. It certainly seems they think father did it. And they won't rest till they find him. God help him if they find him. I only hope the Militia gets there first, before them. For I fear, father won't live, if they find him."

George sat down on the hearth chair and stared into the embers of the fire. He sat for a short time and then got up suddenly. He stood at the window staring at the skies. He studied the clouds that scudded in an amazing pace like wild horses in full gallop across the early afternoon skies. He murmured to himself, "I believe thee to still be alive, father, but where, I do not know. Perhaps it is *my* duty to find out."

Later that morning the endless and blood curdling sound of baying dogs could be heard in the valley. The wind carried the noise all around the area to Sullens where Grace placed her hands over her ears.

"My god, this is a terrible thing to happen. I wish Michal would be found to stop this madness. The noise of those dogs, I can't *bear* it."

"I wonder if he *is* close by?" pondered Ann from her chair by the fire. George was pacing around the parlour, he hands tightly held behind his back, his face pale and sullen.

"He won't be far away, he's no stranger to Newport and that's probably where they'll find him. I wish those hounds would quieten."

"He may be far away; time is running out for him. How could he do this to his own flesh and blood? He must be delirious, he has no respect for any of his kin," said Grace.

George looked towards Grace, "I sometimes wonder how his mind works. I thought I knew my father but now… I believe… I don't know him at all!"

❧

"Why did you do it? I did not mean what I said! You hurt me, nasty man, nasty man, I hate you! Miserable, drunken old man, I despise you, I despise this place you've put me in. Where is Aunt Grace, where is Ann? I'm so scared, help me grandfather, please… I beg you. I am hurting soooo badly!"

Michal woke up terrified in a deathly, cold sweat. He tried to get his bearings; he couldn't remember where he was. As he came to, he realised it was the cave, dark and cold with the wind blowing through the nearby trees, rustling eerily making Michal's imagination race. He called out into the darkness.

"I am so sorry, James. I did not mean it. You spoke bad of me, you pushed my temper. I did not mean to hurt you!" Michal pleaded to the pitiful wailing that his mind could hear that echoed around the cave.

"I despise you grandfather, my wounds are painful, so very painful," came the voice again.

"Go away James…please!" Michal looked wildly about him "Don't you think I've suffered enough. Look what I will be going through when they find me."

"Grandmother despises you too and Mamma. They hate you for what you did to me. They don't want to see you… ever!" The voice persisted.

Michal closed his eyes in remorse. He tried to reason with the voice in his head, but it spoke no more. He lay back down on the ground and tried to get back to sleep.

Dawn brought relief to everyone at Sullens. It had been a long and restless night and George awoke to find Grace sitting at the end of their bed. Her hair was half tied, the other half hung loose over her left shoulder. He reached out to her and touched her.

"Grace, how long have you been there?" he asked, rubbing his eyes.

"Too long, my dearest. I feel I shall never sleep soundly again," replied Grace quietly. She teased a strand of her hair from her face and looked towards the door. The sunlight played against the window as the birds began their eternal choruses.

"You will, in time, you will, we've all had a terrible shock," said George getting up and walking round the room.

"Where is your father? Sleeping I've no doubt. The only concern he'll show is for that wretched cottage. How will you break the news to him?"

"I wish I knew where he could be found," replied George.

Grace glared at him.

"Do you mean he's *still* out there?" she cried out incredulously.

"Yes. Although he *is* my father and I do adore him, I feel Norris is right. He has some doing in this terrible deed." George awaited Grace's response.

She stared in silence, her hands began to tremble. At length she whispered.

"Then there is no question about it."

George nodded in agreement.

"It all makes sense. Everything shows father must be involved."

He held Grace close to him and he began to silently weep.

℘

Deep in the sanctuary of the wood, Michal had been out collecting berries to eat when he first heard the sound of the dogs. His hair stood on end when he realised the manhunt had begun. He grabbed a branch and ripped it from a hazel tree and began to sweep the branch across the ground to disguise his footprints, thrashing dead leaves over his trail back to the cave. When he returned he crawled to the very back of the cave and cowered to the darkest spot and hid in silence. He could still hear the dogs and the occasional voice that was carried by the wind. He had spent the worse night of his life in the cave, the spirits inside his mind had tormented him to the brink of insanity, the wind had played tricks upon his imagination and the dampness was beginning to chill him into the bone.

"How I wish, it was another day, another year, another time," he mumbled to himself, "I wish that James was here, God…please help me!" Michal clenched his hands together and began to beat at his heart.

He spent what seemed like hours just sitting and waiting in the sordid black silence. He could feel insects crawling through his clothes and he thrashed at them desperately to rid his torture. He believed it was God's slow and purposeful punishment that was being inflicted upon him.

Night fell and Michal felt a cramp in his leg so he stood up to relieve the shooting pain. He walked towards the entrance of the cave to get some fresh air. He was desperately hungry and in need of water which he had been without since the night before. At length, he decided he had to venture out from his hiding place, he had to get a drink and the only place he could think of was back at the remains of the cottage near the entrance to the wood. Thirst overcame his mind. He heard the dogs no more so he began his mission.

The wood seemed different at night, Michal knew his way well but, in his current state of mind, he managed to take the wrong direction. Without light he was powerless to convince himself he would soon reach the cottage. He eventually found himself at the other side of Downend. He stared in disbelief as he saw the dimly lit lantern swaying at the Hare and Hounds Inn. Stupidity made him stumble toward the Inn, toward the familiar and welcoming sight. He reached the back door without being seen and peered through one of the windows and saw the place full of villagers all laughing and enjoying a good night's ale. How Michal longed to join them, how he wished he could be one to taste the sweet nectar from a jar. Reality overcame him as he realised what he was doing so he made his way to the water trough used by the horses. Hidden from view he gulped as much water as he could take, strands of grass that had been laying on the water surface caught in his dry throat making him choke, he spat them to the floor. After taking his fill, Michal crept away, looking over his shoulder at every step, looking for signs of the dogs and the Militia as he made his way back to his hideout. He felt it would be safe to travel back along Coach Lane. At every noise he heard he threw himself into the hedges but each time it was his imagination running away with him. He reached the cottage and stopped briefly and stared at the burnt outline of the ruin.

"My dear cottage, oh… Beth, forgive me. I am so sorry," he sadly uttered.

"Not as sorry as you *think,* Morey!" came a gruff voice from the darkness in the lane. "You are under arrest for the murder of James Dove and for arson!"

"No!" screamed Michal horrified, "Noooooo!"

It was too late; Michal felt many hands restraining his struggles as he tried to escape their grasps. He fought like an animal for freedom but the hands overpowered his fatigued body and he sank to the ground. He felt chains being bound around his hands and feet, looped around his neck he felt the chill of iron tighten constricting his breathing.

"Next stop for you is to the gallows, Morey!" came the gruff voice again from the shadows. "Come on, move! You are up for it now…..!"

❧

George had left Sullens and made his way to where he could hear the sound of the mob still searching for Michal. They had been out all day and most of the night, resting only to take in food and drink. George reached Pan Wood and walked towards a group of men huddled together in a corner. It seemed odd to be at his father's work place without the smell of wood smoke or the sound of axe upon wood. No sign of the old man toiling amongst the trees.

The group heard George's approach and turned in his direction, brandishing their "weapons".

One of them called out.

"Surprised to see you ere, Morey. Looking for your old man are ye? Don't have to come too far to do that. You're too late. They *got* him!"

George stared in horror at the group. He moved towards them, pushing them forcibly out of his way. He walked towards another group of men, some restraining their dogs on thick, leather leashes. He could see several members of the local Militia walking back from a darkened area of the wood. They had a man bound in chains within their confines. George gasped in horror as he saw the downtrodden figure of his father being dragged along.

"Oh, my god! Father! Where have you been?" he called out.

He was ushered out of the way by one of the Militia.

"He's been arrested. Hiding out in the old hermit's cave. Barely alive, by the state of him," one of the officers informed George.

"Pray, where are you taking him?" George asked staring at the state of Michal, hardly recognising him.

"To Newport for the time being, then who knows after that," was the curt response. "Probably to Winchester Gaol!"

"Father! It's me, George. Can you hear me?" George desperately tried to keep up with the group of Militia that were dragging Michal to a cart waiting to transport him away.

Michal didn't utter a word. He was exhausted, cold and hungry. At that particular time, he wasn't able to comprehend what was happening to him, let alone realise that his son was at his side.

"Say goodbye to your father, George," Richard Norris appeared from the back of the group of Militia, looking triumphant at his discovery.

"Happy now are ya Norris? Got what you wanted have ya?" George scoffed in disgust at Richard.

"Justice will be done, Morey. He's guilty, for god's sake, *look* at him! He's covered in blood, his clothes, his hair. He stinks of smoke. He's a broken man, what *more* do you need to see that he's a *murderer*?" Richard demanded in annoyance at George's disbelief.

George pretended not to hear as he watched his father pushed up into the waiting cart and taken immediately away in the direction of Newport. He stood helplessly as the mob gradually dispersed back to Arreton. Gossiping incessantly about their find and what would befall the luckless woodcutter.

"So what happens to him now?" asked Grace when George broke the news to her shortly afterwards.

"They've taken him to Newport. I will go there now and try to find out what will happen to father. He's a broken man, Grace. It was terrible to see," George said sadly, thinking of his father bound in chains.

Grace placed her arms around her stricken husband. She hugged him tightly and said, "Think of poor James, think of that poor little boy. Your father; we must think of him too, but why kill the boy?"

Michal was pushed toward a waiting cart and bundled into the back where a foot held his head to the floor, disabling his movements completely. He again heard voices in the dark,

"It was so easy, we just waited until dusk and he appeared like a phantom from hell!"

"Good work everyone!" said a voice that Michal instantly recognised as Richard Norris.

"Norris!" Michal could not believe his ears, "You bastard, how dare you do this to me, I'll get you, mark my words, you're a dead man!"

"You can't hurt me Morey, its only words, you're for it now!" Scoffed Richard Norris, his outline could only just be made out from the darkness. "One way journey!"

"Where are…you… takin' me?" quivered Michal at length.

"You'll be taken to a holding cell tonight in Newport then whatever the law decides to do with you. God only knows that Morey. You'll be up in front of the Judge soon that is for sure and no doubt the gallows after that." A different voice cackled aloud, menacing and mocking.

When they reached Newport, Michal was pushed out of the cart to the ground and dragged to his feet by his captors and ushered into the Gaol. Inside he was shoved into a cell, one of the captors yelled "I hope you *rot* in hell Morey, you deserve it!"

༼༽

Michal kept his eyes tightly shut in fear of what fate would behold him next. He was woken at dawn by the sound of keys rattling in the lock of his cell. He groaned as he felt his wrists aching with the chains still tightly bound, the iron had cut deep into his flesh. He heard the same menacing voice as last night call out, "Morey, there's someone to see you. Must be mad wanting to visit a murder!" it scorned.

"Father!" called a familiar voice.

Michal opened his eyes to see George stood in the doorway.

"Boy! What are you doing here?" he asked.

"To see how you are," said George looking at his father lying on the cold floor of the cell.

"Where are they taking me?" asked Michal trying to get comfortable.

"First to the judge and then to Winchester Prison, you're to sail later this morn. The constable told me you were here; I came as soon as I could."

"You are good to me boy, more than I deserve." Michal looked up at George.

"Are you in much pain, father?" asked George looking very concerned.

"Yes, but no more than I deserve boy…no more," Michal moved his wrists and winced in pain.

"They say I must go now, but I'll try to see you again father." George moved towards the door and stopped

"Before I do, I must know, did you do it…. kill….. James I mean?"

Michal bowed his head; the lack of response was answer enough to George. He turned away and quietly left.

"God bless you boy, look after Grace!" called Michal as he saw George disappear from the cell. He sank back to the floor and wept like a child.

"Hush that row Morey, think how that boy felt when you murdered him," growled the gaoler.

"You don't know I did it, no one knows I did it!" persisted Michal angrily.

"Oh we *know* all right, Morey, there's no doubt you are a killer!" The gaoler slammed the door shut plunging Michal back into darkness again.

∽

Not long after, he was taken to the judge and the decision was made to have him shipped to Winchester to await trial. The turbulent voyage across the Solent from the Island made Michal sick to his stomach as the vessel rose and fell over torrid waves. From his position in the ship he could see his beloved homeland slowly disappearing into the horizon. He clung to the cage in which he was held captive as the two guards that accompanied him laughed and scorned at the woodcutter.

"You should have burnt as well Morey save us this trouble of a journey to t'other side! God knows it would have been a better end to you!"

Michal turned his head away in shame away from their scoffing and mockery. He watched the Island finally disappear from sight as his fate drew ever closer.

CHAPTER TWELVE

The prison horse and cart finally reached Winchester Prison after a very long journey on the road. Michal glanced at the large foreboding building that was masked by a mass of high iron railings that lay about the perimeter high above the tallest roofs. The prison was, as he had feared, menacing, full of evil men, a place no one of any decency would ever come near. Michal was pushed sharply from the back of the cart when it stopped outside the front gates.

"Out you get Morey, hurry along now!" Snarled the guard.

One of them kicked him in the stomach and he winced in pain. His temper frayed. He turned on the guard and growled, "Don't you hit me anymore, or you'll end up in pain, like me boy!"

"Words can't harm me Morey, try this!" The guard kicked Michal high under the ribs making him drop to his knees immediately.

"Get up old man, I said get up!" yelled the guard.

Michal stayed on the floor, winded and unable to move he tried to catch his breath. He felt a blow to his neck, the pain burnt like hot ash. He stumbled to his feet, amidst his pain and humiliation he whispered, "Can't you...stop, leave...me be."

"Move Morey or you'll regret it!" came the angry reply from the guard who had now lost his temper.

"The only thing I regret is being alive," said Michal trying to ease the pain on his neck but his hands would not reach as the chains still bit into his wrists. The guard pushed Michal roughly towards the gates of the prison.

"Inside Morey, hope you like your new home, nice and cosy. You'll be looked after!" The guard cackled in hysterical laughter.

Ignoring the comments, Michal shuffled inside the gates; the pain in his body was intense and continuous. He was led through a dark passage, which was illuminated only by candles near the entrance. As they walked through Michal could hear the prison inmates. Their cries of help, cries from madmen, vagrants and thieves. He reached his cell that was no bigger than the cart he had travelled in; there he was greeted by a strong smell of excreta permeating the stale air.

"Enjoy your stay Morey!" The guard laughed as he shoved Michal inside and slammed the door and locking it. Michal felt his way to the back of the cell; he felt something brush past his arm. He turned in the darkness and could just make out a human shape against the window. There was another shape alongside of the first.

A voice said, "Welcome to hell, brother. If you survive longer than a week then you are doing well here."

Michal turned away from the voice. He spoke through the dark.

"How long have you been in here?" he asked.

"A week tomorrow, brother, but tomorrow will tell if I am to survive," returned the gruff but friendly voice.

The second voice spoke suddenly. "There have been two die here this week," entering into the conversation without being prompted.

"One died of the torture; the other, well lets say we helped him along."

Michal shuddered and leant against the wall as the gruff voice asked, "What is your crime brother?"

Michal paused, her heard feet shuffling impatiently awaiting for his reply, "I… murdered… a boy," He muttered.

"Oh, you *are* a bad boy then are you? A bad boy like me. The only difference is I've murdered five, yes, five and I enjoyed it. I love to kill, don't you brother?" The voice informed him.

Michal could hear the change in the voice as it relived the thoughts of its crimes; it broke into a ghoulish laughter. Michal didn't answer; he remained at the back of the cell, far as possible from the voices that continued to cackle at odd intervals. He didn't want any trouble, his body ached enough from the treatment from the guards. He crouched slowly to the floor amongst a few patches of straw. It was cold and damp with the smell of sweat and excreta that overpowered the whole cell. Michal prayed for sunlight so he could take a glimpse of his fellow prisoners. He decided it best not to sleep in case the other two may choose to attack him, so he vigilantly kept awake. He felt himself dozing on several occasions and hours later to his relief that he heard gentle snoring coming from the other side of the cell so he bent his head and drifted off to sleep himself.

❧

Days passed into weeks as Michal became accustomed to his dreadful surroundings that were only marginally better than that of the cave at Downend. During the previous week one of the prisoners in Michal's cell had been taken away and executed at Portsmouth for the murders he had committed. The other prisoner, Leyland, remained. His crime, Michal learned was that of horse stealing in the New Forest. Michal found this man to be fairly decent and he spent a lot of time talking about his life and of his crime. Leyland listened with interest as Michal told him how James had provoked the attack.

"You must have felt strongly to have murdered the boy," he replied at length.

"Yes, I did, enough to kill him. I never felt the way as I did then, I heard the voices telling me inside my head to do it, and I did, I tried to stop it but I couldn't," said Michal as he relived the experience.

"So you are for the gallows, my friend?" questioned Leyland.

"I believe that to be my fate," said Michal "I am trying to prepare for the day, but how long I am to be here, I do not know."

"They'll keep you guessing," said Leyland, "one day you'll be dragged off, never to be seen again. Same with me, my crime befits hanging. It was born in me to thieve. My father was the same, always stole, always horses, but I never killed a man; I just couldn't do that."

"Believe me I didn't want the boy to die. No one else will believe me except perhaps my son, George. I wish I could tell him what happened."

"Do you think he'll venture here?" asked Leyland rubbing his legs as cramp filled them.

"Don't know, I would like to see him once again though," said Michal, "just once more."

∾

The weeks turned into months as the Prison tightly held the woodcutter within its walls. The prisoners were only allowed out of their cells once a week to get some fresh air outside and to stretch their limbs. Michal's health had suffered badly. He had developed a severe cough and deep, penetrating pains in his shoulders which were already riddled with rheumatism and arthritis. He spent each cold night lying on the damp floor with just a handful of straw for his comfort. One afternoon Leyland was taken away from the cell. When he left he bid farewell to Michal and, as he did so he, turned and said.

"Just remember, it comes to us all."

And with those words he left the prison to his impending doom.

A week later, Michal was gazing through the tiny window in the cell when he heard his voice called by the Gaoler, "Morey, visitor for Morey!"

Michal stumbled to the door, as he heard the key turn the lock and open his jaw dropped. There was George standing in the passage. He looked pale and frightened as Michal approached him.

"George! How good it is to see you, how are you boy!"

"Well… father, how are you? How are you coping in this hole?" asked George looking about him.

"Well it's rough and smells bad but, they feed me, what else can I say. How is Grace and what of Sullens?"

"Grace is fine, she is coping well. She's found work about a month ago, in a kitchen."

"Oh," said Michal bleakly, "What other news is there? It's been so long."

"Talk has died down now. The people have stopped their idle gossip some time ago. Although some of them don't talk to us at all," said George.

"What of the cottage?" asked Michal quietly, not daring to look at his son.

"The ruin is still there, untouched since the fire. You look tired, father." George looked at Michal and at how ill he was looked.

"I've bought you some thing to eat, some garnish, to keep you strong. I wish now I had come earlier. I had no idea what this place was like, I won't forget it now."

"Thanks boy, yes it's hard, but I am so glad to see you," Michal smiled, the first time for an age. Taking the basket of food he began to eat hungrily. Among mouthfuls he added, "You spoil your old father, how I am enjoying every morsel of this fare."

"When do you go for trial father?" asked George hesitantly.

"I've been told nothin'. I try to live each day as best I can. I know the day is soon to come when I am tried, but until that day I try not to think of it."

George looked at his father and asked spoke outright.

"You did do it, didn't you father? I have to know."

Michal stayed silent gulping a mouthful of food, looking at George he eventually said, "I did not mean for the boy to die. I just wanted to scare him."

"What did he do to you to make you *kill* him?" asked George in amazement.

"He was rude, to me, to Ann. He kept saying I was a drunken idiot, words I won't hear of, not from anyone." Michal's eyes flashed in anger.

George stretched out his hand and touched his father's arm.

"He made me so angry," continued Michal, "an anger that welled up inside me like never before and then… and… then I brought that axe down upon him. I think he was dead after the first blow. I can't remember it's all a daze now but I do remember being out of control, I drove that blade maybe a dozen times to his body. Then I saw him lying there, in the grass not moving and then I knew… what I'd done."

"But what made you burn the cottage down?" asked George in no more than a whisper. He turned away from his father and put a hand to his head in disbelief. He rubbed his eyes miserably, unable to comprehend what his father was telling him.

"I had to get rid of the body somehow. I panicked, I had to hide, get away," said Michal quickly.

"Where did you hide then?" asked George.

"In a cave by the wood, near the clearing, it was horrible, the voices were there. Then the dogs, that meant my fate was upon me and then I was found and brought here, the rest you know."

"The boy did nothing to harm you though did he, father?" George put a hand to his head.

"Not in so many ways boy, no he didn't hurt me. It was just the way he always asked for something and got it handed on a plate. I have always wanted a life like that of James Dove. I was denied any happiness in my life. I suppose I envied the boy. I don't know… I just don't know anymore. Anyway my life is over. You had better go, boy." Michal felt tears in his eyes as he blinked them away.

George looked sadly at his father.

"I must get back, the boat sails soon back to the Island." He walked towards Michal and hugged him tightly. He held the tired old woodcutter for the last time. Michal felt a lump welling up in his throat and tears fell from his eyes.

"Goodbye my son… and thank you," he whispered.

George left the prison in silence, Michal watched him go through the bars of his window until he could see him no longer. He returned to the corner of the cell, kneeling down he prayed to God for the sake of his family.

ے

Dawn broke the next morning bringing heavy rainfall. Small drops of water spattered through the cell window waking Michal. He stretched and rubbed his shoulder and heard the gaoler walking along the passage chinking the keys with each step. The gaoler was early that morning. Michal heard the keys turn in his lock.

"Come on Morey; stir yourself you are on trial this morning. I have orders to take you to the court building now," announced the gaoler, with a smirk on his face.

Michal stumbled forward, today was to be his day of reckoning. The gaoler bound Michal with chains over his wrists.

"Come on, we're to go now," he said.

He led Michal through the passage, the rain beat against the roof and the moans from the other prisoners and the clinking of his chains seemed to beat a solemn rhythm as he trudged along. Michal felt his legs beginning to give way beneath him. The gaoler steadied his balance.

"Come on old man, you won't be coming back here again."

"So this is it then, this is to be my trial?" asked Michal. He needed to hear from someone to confirm his fears.

"That is right, Morey. You probably know your fate already."

"I have a good idea," said Michal sadly. He felt sick and anxious and wished he was already dead.

"It is a swift business from what I hear," said the gaoler as he directed Michal towards the waiting cart. "The journey is not long," he added.

"Just one thing," said Michal before he clambered into the cart. "If my son George comes, can you please tell him that I cared for him, with all my heart and that I never meant to cause all this trouble?"

"I will," said the gaoler solemnly, "now come on, away with you."

ഇ

The cart arrived at the court building carrying the bewildered and frightened Michal after a brief journey. He was taken to a chamber where he was placed into a large cage at the side of the dock. He glanced about him and saw a sea of faces staring back at him. Suddenly, the judge entered the chamber, seated himself and peered around the room. He looked towards Michal.

"You are Michal Morey of Downend in the parish of Arreton. You are on trial for the murder of one James Dove, your grandson in June in the year of our Lord, 1736 and for the burning down of your cottage in Coach Lane. It has been recorded at the vestry meeting at Arreton Parish that you are guilty of murdering of James Dove. What have you to say?"

Michal stared blankly at the judge.

"I have nothing to say," he bowed his head to the floor.

The judge glared back at Michal.

"Are you guilty or not guilty of the murder of James Dove?"

Again Michal remained calm and again he announced.

"I have the guilt of ten fold; I know I must now pay for my crime."

The judge turned to the court, donned a black cap and announced.

"I hereby find Michal Morey of Downend in the parish of Arreton, Isle of Wight, guilty of the murder of James Dove. I sentence you to death. You will be removed from this court and at high noon be hung by the neck until dead."

ↄ

The chamber exploded into a mass of voices and shrieks of delight at the spectacle of a public hanging. Michal bowed his head as the guards dragged him to the court cells below the chamber. He could hear a buzz of a crowd outside and he sat in silence, his mind clear of any thoughts. He was called for just before noon and taken outside to the wooden scaffold, which was to be his place of execution. The rain had stopped and sunshine spilt into the courtyard hurting Michal's eyes with the strength of its rays. Each step he took led him closer to his death as the wooden structure loomed high above his head. All about him people had gathered and were jostling to get the best view. Others stood in every available space, in windows, doorways pushing themselves towards the scaffold. As he approached the steps Michal saw a man standing alone on the structure, he was the man who would end Michal's life. He was the hangman.

Michal gasped as the reality finally hit him and fear rose throughout his body. The guard pushed Michal the first few steps as the crowd surged forward and the jeering began. He heard chants throughout the sea of faces of "*Murderer, child murderer rot in hell!*" The mob then began to throw objects at him. As he stood below the noose above his head, Michal took a deep breath as the hangman placed the noose around his neck. The rope was cold and heavy, its roughness cut into Michal's flesh as the rope tightened around his neck.

"Have you anything to say, Morey?" asked the hangman.

"No, I ….have… nothing… to say," replied Michal.

The hangman turned to the crowd and cried,

"This is Michal Morey found guilty of murder."

As the noise of jeering became deafening,   Michal closed his eyes and began to pray, the hangman raised his hand and released the trap door beneath Michal's feet and he dropped down instantly,   hanging by his neck like a rag doll, his body quivering as the life was sucked from him. The crowd cheered and gradually began to disperse as they callously awaited the next victim for to be hanged. Michal's body was then cut down and placed back into the same cart that had carried him to his execution. It had been agreed that his body be returned to the Island and displayed in such a way that the gravity of his crime would serve as a reminder to others. Michal's body was to be suspended in an iron gibbet and placed at the roadside at Downend on Gallows Hill, as a reminder what may become of others should they commit such a heinous crime.

When the news reached George Morey at Sullens of Michal's execution he was grief stricken. Grace found him in the garden staring towards Pan Wood. She stood by his side and gently whispered, "Come back inside now, its getting late."

"I know it's late…too late," said George distantly.

"I only hope his death was instant. I have news from the prison, from the gaoler who said father wanted me to know that he… cared…. for me."

Grace placed her arms round George's shoulders.

"Although he was a criminal at the end, he was a fine man and good father to his children," she gently reassured him.

"Yes and I will never forget him…ever," George wiped a tear from his face.

"We won't be able to travel too far near the Downs road now will we," said Grace and she shivered as she thought of the body hanging in the gibbet.

"No we won't, but I cannot understand why they want to cause more pain into my heart. Why can't he be laid to rest, he has paid his penalty, is that not enough for the people?" cried George.

"We have no need to go that way," repeated Grace.

"No I will never set foot upon that road there is no fear of that," said George defiantly. "If anyone dare utter one single word to me about father, I shall truly be the next body hanging in a gibbet, for I too will be a murderer!"

"George!" said Grace shocked "don't talk that way!" Her husband's anger began to make her uneasy, he had sounded just like Michal.

"Grace, those words are not spoken by the true George Morey. Please leave me alone for a while, I need to be alone."

"Yes, as you wish my dearest." Grace obediently left George in the garden. As she walked back into the house, she caught sight of him break down into tears. She felt the tears in her own eyes, she knew he needed time; time that she prayed would heal his pain.

CHAPTER

THIRTEEN

It was close on a year since the murder and summer was nearing. The remains of Michal's body were still encased within the gibbet. It was a terrible sight. Rooks had descended and feasted upon the body, grabbing any morsel of flesh that remained, the wind and rain and sun had washed, cleaned and bleached white the remaining bones.

George had decided enough was enough and he went to Arreton to demand that the gibbet be removed and Michal's body buried. A vestry meeting was held at the church and it was decided to have the body taken down as most people were afraid to venture past the spectacle especially as night fell. It was with relief when George told Grace the news.

"At least he can now be finally laid to rest."

"Not before time though. He is to be buried on Gallows Hill this afternoon. I am going to pay my last respects," said George.

"And I will be *right* beside you," said Grace.

George reached out and hugged her. He felt the anguish of the year slowly being lifted from his mind. The pain had been enough to age George since the murder and he realised he was now a much wiser man.

As they stood beside the shallow grave later that afternoon, George uttered a few words and prayed for Michal's soul to be forgiven. Grace laid a small posy of flowers on the grave, as she did so a gust of wind blew them across the grass, she returned to replace them but George held her arm.

"Leave them be Grace, he will not mind. Nothing matters to him anymore, he is at rest. Let us go now."

ᛒ

George held Grace's arm as they slowly walked away from the graveside. The wind howled relentlessly through the trees in Coach Lane as they walked back to Sullens. The leaves rustled as they walked past the foliage-encrusted copse. George looked over towards it.

"Perhaps he's back at work now amongst his beloved wood, cutting trees."

Grace looked at her husband and didn't reply. She knew Michal would never be far away not even in the spirit world that he now existed in.

They carried on walking until they reached the cottage. Its remains still stood but now were covered in ivy that had taken a stranglehold on the existing stone walls. They stopped and stared at the cottage. At length, George spoke.

"We will never know how much he loved that place. It must have broken his heart to have set fire to it; to destroy it and the memories of mother."

"He was a sad and very lonely man, George. He died when your mother died. He always admitted that. Life had no real meaning to him. And, with James, we all hoped he would stir himself and start to live again…but he never did." Grace held onto George's arm.

"Come, let's leave this place…" George urged Grace to move forward.

ↄ

They continued to walk along the road and as they neared Sullens, Richard Norris walked towards them. He nodded his acknowledgement of them in silence. George stopped him in his path.

"Norris…you were right, father was guilty."

Richard stared at George for a while.

"I'm sorry, George. I always knew he was guilty. He had that ability…he always had that ability to be able to do something so bad…I'm sorry it was young James that was the victim. He had so much to live for and…now…" he broke off.

"I wish you no ill, Richard. In spite of it all…" returned George and offered his hand towards Richard.

Richard shook it in gratitude.

"Thanking you, George. I wish you and your family good health and happiness and an end to the torment and sadness you have had. I only wish your mother was here to be with you…I only wish…"

He limped away, desperate to hide the tears that welled in his eyes as he thought of Beth. Although he was a man reaching mid-life, he missed her so much and the torment of seeing her home burnt to the ground was a constant reminder to him.

❧

George and Grace continued to live at Sullens for many years to come and, on some lonely, quiet nights, they were sure they could hear the woodcutter labouring away in the wood. The distinct chopping of an axe would echo eerily across the valley almost as though Michal had never gone away.

ABOUT THE AUTHOR

Harriet J Kent is a born and bred Islander of many generations. Her ancestors were predominantly from the farming community on the Isle of Wight.

This is Harriet's first novel which she has enjoyed writing as it involves her beloved Isle of Wight. Harriet runs her own secretarial services based in Newport. She lives with her husband Paul, along with Lucy and Misty, the Jack Russells.

Printed in the United Kingdom
by Lightning Source UK Ltd.
122686UK00001B/133-159/A